Reviews

"A terrific book, *Living Yes* is a program full of wisdom that allows readers to live authentically and embrace whatever life circumstances they are currently facing. Mark Morris's personal and clinical wisdom come through loud and clear in his witty and accessible writing. *Living Yes* is a must-read for anyone striving for personal growth and quality of life."

—Amy Wenzel, PhD, Psychologist and Author of
Strategic Decision Making in Cognitive Behavioral Therapy

"Instead of psycho-babble, cliff notes, or simplistic pep talks, *Living Yes* gives solid and relevant skills that can help you feel better – if you put in the effort. It is a rare book in this regard."

—Michael Tofani, MD, Psychiatrist

"Mark Morris clearly reveals the keys taught to mental health practitioners. By Living Yes as Mark describes, nearly anyone can use these ideas to feel more happy and alive."

—Ronald E. Marks, PhD, Dean, Tulane University School of Social Work

"In *Living Yes*, Mark Morris offers a blueprint to a happier and more meaningful life. As a doctor for more than 30 years, I notice that at least a quarter of my patients are suffering from emotional distress which causes symptoms and hinders care. *Living Yes* is clear, enlightened, and empowering to the core. If all my patients would read this book, I would have more time to put down my prescription pad and pick up my fishing pole."

—Richard D. Kagen, MD, Primary Care Physician

Testimony

(What students of the Living Yes program have to say. To read more testimony, visit www.LivingYes.org.)

"My son and I have settled down. I want to get out of bed in the morning. Learned I can't control what's not in my power."

"I was told I was gonna lose my leg to diabetes and I accepted it with no reaction, thanks to Living Yes. I didn't even lose sleep over it. That never would have happened before."

"Before Living Yes, I used to feel really alone and all over the place with my feelings. I didn't realize that I am worthy of love and respect. It's OK to be who I am."

"I used to think I was ugly, but now I think I'm beautiful."

"I used to get angry with organizations, blame myself for all my failures, not express myself to others. I now know I have tools to help calm me, feel good about myself, take life with a positive attitude."

"I was afraid of the world, could not speak up, could not go out without a drink or pill. Now I see my life totally differently now that I'm Living Yes. I got back in my church and also attend school. My wife thinks I am a new changed man."

"Living Yes has helped me grow into a much better father, brother, son and mentor. Living Yes has taught me to be more open to love and embrace new beginnings."

"I have more peace because I'm not controlling everything. I relate to people better. I used to be angry every day, but now I can sit and listen to my wife most of the time without getting angry."

LIVING YES

A Handbook for Being Human

Mark Morris, MSW, MFA

LIVING YES, a Handbook for Being Human

Morris, Mark
      Living Yes : A Handbook for Being Human

Published by Amirh Voice
www.AmirhVoice.com

ISBN 978–0692340264

Info@LivingYes.org
www.LivingYes.org

Book design by Anna Gilbert-Duveneck

Dedicated to K. Bradford Brown, Ph. D., 1929-2007
Everyone he met knew they were special.

"Play wrong and make that right." Thelonious Monk

Contents

Introduction: *Living Yes or Dying No?*   2

Chapter One: *How to Live Yes*   11

Chapter Two: *Learning Acceptance*   25

Chapter Three: *Setting Boundaries and Sticking with Them*   40

Chapter Four: *The Voice in Your Head*   53

Chapter Five: *Feelings and Thoughts*   74

Chapter Six: *Feeling Emotions*   95

Chapter Seven: *Patterns of No*   119

Chapter Eight: *Some Practical Ideas*   137

Chapter Nine: *Finding Peace*   149

Chapter Ten: *Putting It Together*   169

Detailed Contents *(with Headings and Sub-headings)*   178

Splash!

If I gave you ten million dollars to dive into freezing glacier water, would you? What if I offered you ten million dollars to read this book carefully, do all the exercises, and then Live Yes to the best of your ability? Would you? What if I sweetened the offer by adding a satisfying job, a loving relationship, the ability to choose fun freely, and freedom from being overwhelmed by painful emotions? Would you jump in? Now, what if by reading this book you could gain the freedom to *not* desire the ten million dollars, but you could still create everything else? Would you still read it and go for Living Yes? If so, dive in and get ready to make a splash!

Introduction: Living Yes or Dying No?

ARE YOU LIVING YES OR DYING NO?

What have you been taught?

What does the title *Living Yes, a Handbook for Being Human* mean? This will be easier to answer by looking at what Living Yes is not. My friend Jeff pointed out that the opposite of Living Yes would be "Dying No." The opposite of Living Yes could also be "Stuck No," "Tight-gripped No," "Dried-out No," "Pissed-off No," "Closed-hearted No." Isn't this how most people approach their lives? Don't most people reject everything they don't like until they shrivel and become numbed-out, anger-stuffed, worrying zombies who are stuck thinking "No" in response to everything that they don't like? We fight and get angry or hide and avoid anything that makes us uncomfortable. And we keep at it, unless we learn a better way

When we were young children, we naturally lived Yes, but as we grew up, we were exposed to family misbehaviors, domestic violence, mental violence, hatred, anger, jealousy, crazy TV news, political failure, office power games, relationship conflicts, physical pain, losing our creativity, and on and on. Over the years we tightened into a defensive crouch. We can present a smile or have a few people in our lives with whom we feel safe, but the overall trend is to be stuck in No. To feel better, we race after anything that excites or relaxes us.

Fight, flight, or freeze is not the only way to respond to what greets us in our lives. Instead of resisting and struggling, we can learn to change our thinking. We can choose practical ways to move to a fresher, creative, and, dare I say, more enlightened course. We can give up being rigid and move with the tide. We can learn what lessons the sea is teaching, go beyond the wave, and become part of the entire ocean. Instead of drowning in No, we can learn from it, get its message, and become part of the flow. I hope you'll read on, dive in, and choose to Live Yes.

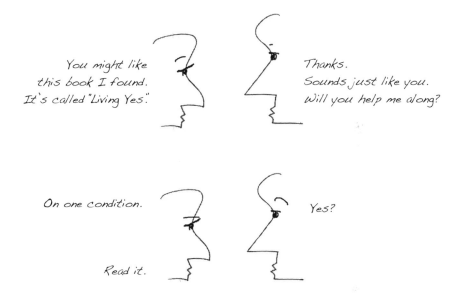

BEING HUMAN

Human is what I am. No more. No less.

While stuck in our No, we have lost sight of what it means to be human. In fact, we no longer know what human means. Brad Brown taught that to be human is to be lovable, real, and limited.

We have lost sight of our lovability when we believe harsh words that others say about us. We retreat and change ourselves in unhealthful ways because of the meanings we put on the events in our lives. We have forgotten that we are loveable.

We hide in pretend worlds, making our own versions of

reality. We watch people puff themselves up so others will believe they are important. We puff ourselves up in return. They see that and pretend to be who they are not, and the cycle continues. We have been taught to pretend in order to get ahead, to get promoted, to get elected. Our leaders and our selves fail because we cannot live up to the fake identities we are working so hard to show. But being real is always available.

Our power comes from knowing our own limits. When we play God and work to manipulate everything, we fail. We control only what is within our abilities. When we focus our energies only on what we can influence, we will succeed.

Being human means we are realizing our lovability, our realness, and the limits of our humanness. When we think we are unlimited, we are dead wrong. True power comes from being genuine and humble. That is what it means to be human.

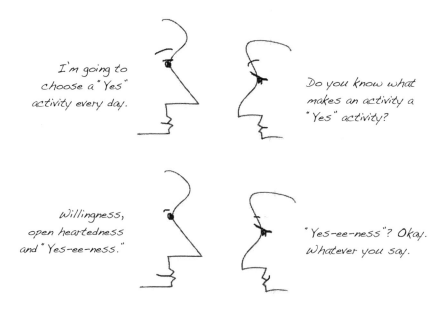

Take a breath. Look at where your mind is now. And when you're ready, ask this question:

Do I want a huge leap forward in my power and appreciation for Life?

The answer to this question must be Yes. That means now, this very moment, is your first chance to choose to Live Yes. Take a stand that your life does not have to be a rough and tumble of habit and pain. Assert your willingness to find your personal freedom. Live Yes by allowing the possibility that there may be something to learn about your life ahead that you don't already know. Have a clear intention and put yourself in the presence of others with the same clear intention. If you are willing, you have an opportunity to find the power to release your own joy. If you want to learn how to Live Yes, then read on.

ABOUT THE BOOK

How does this book work?

Living Yes is a simple book but not an easy one. The language is basic, so anyone may learn the material.

The book is loaded with ideas in the way a funny movie is loaded with jokes. You may not get them all, but you will be offered many chances to become inspired. Take the time to pause and think about these ideas. Look at how you are living your life and how you might make changes.

All self-help books are about change. Living Yes is a way to make change at every decision point in your life. Most self-help books are about something specific, such as depression, anxiety, weight loss, money, personality, communication, career, or relationships. *Living Yes* is about all these. It is filled with big ideas.

Living Yes unlocks the code for learning from life. Except for mental health professionals, few possess the knowledge given on these pages. The book blends cognitive theory, modern change movements, the twelve steps, spiritual traditions, and mindfulness all into one simple approach. Thanks to *Living Yes,* the secret's out!

Some believe that figuring out who we are and how we got this way is all we need. But that is not quite enough to Live Yes. We need a set of techniques that will reveal our resistance (find the No) and then accept the core truth of the situation (Live Yes). That's what the exercises offer. The exercises are the key to mastering the magic of Living Yes.

Everything worthwhile requires discipline. If you look through *Living Yes* quickly and then put it on the shelf, you may miss the chance to learn to Live Yes. If you approach the book with an "I'll try" attitude instead of an "I will" attitude, you may miss the chance to learn to Live Yes. If you expect to "get it" all at once, you may miss the chance to learn to Live Yes.

Sometimes you may notice that you are reading an idea that seems similar to something you have already read. This is excellent. It is how the book reinforces important ideas. It also means you are getting it.

Some parts of the text are likely to grab you – make you wonder, feel, remember, and rebel. When you look at the book again later, those parts may not rub you any longer because you've mastered them, but a different part may still get you. This is normal. It's how we grow.

If you use *Living Yes* as a handbook for being human, freedom is your reward. *Living Yes* is a handbook because it teaches skills. The exercises in this book are powerful. Take the time to read the text with care. Many of the ideas may seem unusual until you start experiencing the benefits of Living Yes. With time, attention, and practice, these ideas will make sense. And when they make sense, watch out! You will understand more than you ever imagined.

The exercises are sometimes written with more challenging language than the text, as are The Living Yes Principles which follow. They are meant to be more closely studied, so you may get the deepest benefit from them. Do the exercises as well as you can, and let Life take care of the rest. In fact, if you read the text and charts with care and do all the exercises fully, you are Living Yes!

Parts of the book may be confusing at first. Guess what? That's great! If your thinking is being challenged, it means you're growing. If you find something you can't see as true, mark the section and come back later. Test the ideas by experiencing Living Yes every day in your own life.

Many self-help books are packed with entertaining stories. This book does not have those. The story that matters is yours. Instead, the ideas and exercises of *Living Yes* are front and center.

The progress check questions that follow each chapter help you see how well you understand the ideas. They challenge you and encourage you to think about how you can Live Yes. They are a starting place to help you write your own story. Use your answers to the questions to write and talk about how you are Living Yes in your life.

As you've seen, the cartoons create a change of pace and

help reinforce the ideas that are being presented. The young man is doing his best to Live Yes. Can his older sister help him?

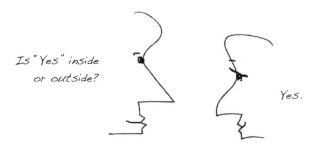

Congratulations. You are about to start a grand adventure. Are you ready? Set to go? Dive!

THE LIVING YES PRINCIPLES
What is Living Yes?

The Living Yes Principles give a full dose of what Living Yes means. After you have completed reading the book, these ideas will be easier to understand. You may want to review them often.

Living Yes begins with observing the behaviors in self and others in various contexts. We learn to recognize how Life itself is providing repeated opportunities for us to Live Yes, based on the ongoing choices we are making.

By observing our emotional response to each of our life's events, we apply insights to identify barriers. We reveal our resistance (find the No) and accept the core truth of the situation (Live Yes).

Living Yes does not mean saying "Yes" to everything, faking positivity, or pretending that what we think is always true. That is avoidance.

Living Yes offers an opportunity to manage our unconscious, automatic reacting. By Living Yes, we overcome such self-destructive habits as blame, resentment, undue anxiety, unnecessary frustration, expectations of fairness, complaining, criticizing, gossiping, or making unnecessary demands on ourselves and on others.

Living Yes means realizing that anger or shame are possible only if we believe in our rigid version of the past, and that there can be no anxiety, worry, or fear if we stop working to control the future.

Living Yes means being honest about our feelings, our distorted thoughts, and our relationship with Life.

Living Yes means we recognize that what we think is not the same as who we are. We engage in the ongoing battle against our falsely held beliefs. We notice our separating responses (find the No), and we identify our constructive behaviors (Live Yes in context). We use our free will to make choices, overcome fate, and create destiny.

Living Yes means we identify the signals and meanings of each event that is offered to us by Life as it is. We accept the lessons of reality. We choose to accept Life's gifts in full, even if we don't like what is being offered and even if we have failed to do so in the past.

When we realize that we have not been "meeting life on Life's terms," we examine our own attitude and accept the lessons of reality that are being offered to us by Life as it is. In our context, we take responsibility to change our attitude and improve our choices.

From awareness, we move forward by accepting what is being offered. We notice and experience our thoughts, feelings, and body sensations. We let go of resistance.

Once we say "Yes," we have chosen our outlook. In each situation that arises, we use the opportunity to stand on our truth by taking concrete action in a values-centered direction.

We continue to Live Yes by moving forward: through faith in what is greater than we are, confidence in our humanity, and bold action resulting from our clarity, while we continuously plumb the deep well of peace.

Living Yes means accepting everything that happened in the past and having zero expectations of the future. This is done by knowing that the present moment is infinite.

Living Yes means we accept our limitations honestly and balance them with our faith in the connectedness of all Life, which is commonly called love. We discover that making this quantum change in ourselves produces a sea change in our world.

Living Yes means we constantly open our hearts and minds to do what our truest inner self is being called to do.

Living Yes means being right here, right now, in all of Life's glories and all of its pains. Those who Live Yes know that suffering is part of the human experience. By Living Yes, we do not become attached to that suffering. Instead we evolve into a new state, which is found in the silence that lies behind the veil of our conscious awareness.

When we Live Yes with deep humility and infinite gratitude, we find ourselves present in a newfound peace, reconnected to our essential self. In order to Live Yes, we must continually discover where we are saying "No," and that is where the work of Living Yes begins.

PROGRESS CHECK

What does it mean for you to be human?

What are your hopes for Living Yes in your own life?

What part of your life do you intend to change for yourself?

Write your personal definition of Living Yes.

Are you ready to read on?

1 How to Live Yes

FORGET BEING POSITIVE

You can't be real if you fake it.

I've decided
to be happy
all the time.

Are you going
to be stupid all
the time, too?

Living Yes is not a book about being positive. It is not about sugar-coating or faking anything. *Living Yes* is a book about telling the truth.

Pushing yourself to hold a falsely positive mood is a temporary and doomed approach to finding the truth. Living Yes means honestly embracing your limits and surrendering to the reality of what Life is offering you at the moment.

I capitalize "Life" when it means a universal gift. By Living Yes, we assume that Life is here to help us learn, change, identify what matters, and find meaning. Some call this faith. Some call it hope. Some call it religion, or God, or Allah, or Vishnu. Some don't call it anything but have learned by experience that Life works for them.

As I said, *Living Yes* is not a book about being positive. *Living Yes* is a book about telling the truth. While being positive has merits, it will not change you when you want to escape what you do not like about yourself.

Living Yes is not a book about religion or faith or assumptions about Life. *Living Yes* is a book that presents a simple and practical approach to finding your own truth. To tell the truth requires trust. Living Yes is built on a foundation of learning to trust that consequences will work out well in the long run.

Many current, popular self-help books say: If you deeply concentrate on a positive result, it will happen. Living Yes does not see the world with this "if you think it, it will come" *(Field of Dreams)* approach. Instead, *Living Yes* starts with the assumption that reality is a gift, and our job is to learn to appreciate the value and meaning of that gift. Life is a school, and no one promised that school would be easy. We can't get an "A" by simply picturing one on our exam. We have to learn the lesson and pass the test. A good school is never a pushover.

Living Yes offers many tools, which we may use to improve our lives and live our values while remaining grounded in this marvelous world. We create a firm footing not with mental magic but with honest work. While prayer, visualization, and self-healing are powerful tools which have their place, we choose to begin within a practical context. We cannot create a world with no problems, where no one gets sick, no one ever dies, there is never any loss, no one is ever mistreated, no one ever gets angry, no one feels scared, and everything is always perfect. To think otherwise is silly.

By living "life on Life's terms," we are accepting an invitation to be fully human. That's the goal. This book lays out a roadmap.

But guess what? If we do Live Yes, we are more likely to end up with the gift of feeling better. We improve our lives. *Living Yes* offers one promise: If you bring yourself into living, you will feel better. Maybe that is a promise of being positive? But, as you know, *Living Yes* is not a book about being positive. Still, if we become more positive by Living Yes, what's the downside?

Live Yes, not as a false positive but as an honest choice. Let's fulfill our responsibilities *and* claim our freedom.

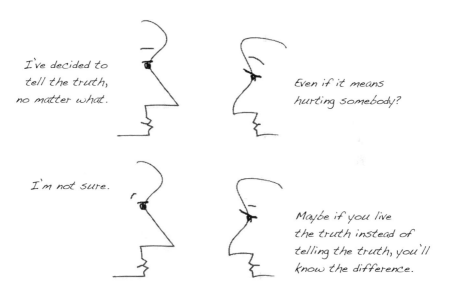

ZERO EXPECTATIONS

Unmet expectations result in frustration.
Instead, expect nothing.

Let's start with a wild idea: Eliminate all expectations. That's right, have zero expectations. The idea to have zero expectations is usually met with resistance or shock.

Please don't push back right away. For now, just consider what it would be like to have zero expectations. (More is written about setting goals and looking at the future later in this chapter and in Chapter Eight.)

The popular serenity prayer used by Alcoholic Anonymous (AA) lays out a way to balance our approach to acceptance and change. In AA it is also taught that "expectations and serenity are inversely proportional."

When we lower our expectations (increase acceptance), our serenity (peace) rises.

And when we have zero expectations, we feel complete serenity.

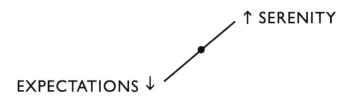

When we expect an outcome and it doesn't happen, Life hits us on the head. Failed expectations result in frustration or disappointment. When expectations are not met, we often fight and say "No" to the experience. These feelings of frustration or disappointment offer us a clue that points to a Life lesson. Live by the saying "That which does not kill me can make me stronger."

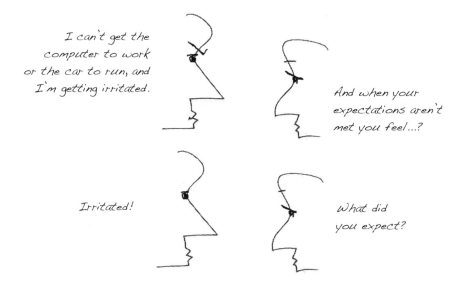

I can't get the computer to work or the car to run, and I'm getting irritated.

And when your expectations aren't met you feel...?

Irritated!

What did you expect?

AM I A SELFISH KNOW-IT-ALL?

The more you think you know, the less you can learn.

Life requires us to believe in possibility outside of ourselves. If we "know it all" we become trapped in our selfishness. If we "know it all," we are taking over the role of our Higher Power. If we "know it all," we leave no opportunity to learn, grow, or improve. If we "know it all," we end up with a life of increasing frustration and selfishness. To believe that the world should conform to our personal view causes us extra pain. Instead, meet life on Life's terms and explore the possibility of a human solution that is outside of your old beliefs.

When you hide your selfish beliefs, you start pretending. You mask your disappointments with false smiles and false praise. You hide your shame behind such things as clothes, cars, and food. And you keep telling others how to live even though you may have lost your own compass. When people see you pretend, they don't connect with you, and you are left alone and separated.

That loneliness reinforces your belief that the world is cruel and scary. A little pretending creates a little distance. A lot of pretending creates fear and isolation. Pretending to "know it all" can only end with you being alone.

EXPECTATIONS AND REALITY

When reality does not meet your expectations,
you become annoyed.

The farther our expectations are from reality, the more separated we become from reality. This gap shows itself through emotions such as frustration, rage, anger, annoyance, disappointment, and sadness. Look at this chart:

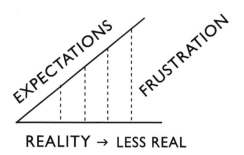

The graph shows that as our expectations move farther from reality, we feel more frustration. At the point (on the lower left corner) where expectations and reality meet, we have zero expectations and zero frustration. However, the farther our expectations separate from reality (moving up and right), the more frustrated (or sad or anxious) we become. To find peace, eliminate all expectations.

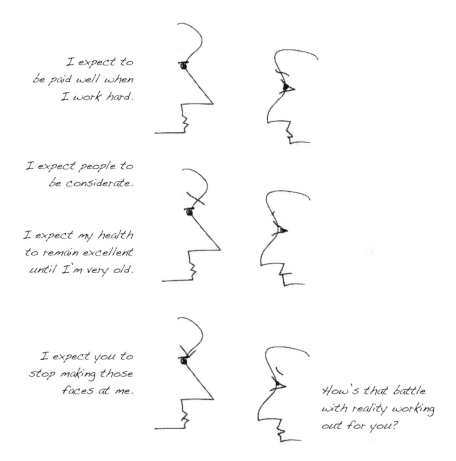

I expect to
be paid well when
I work hard.

I expect people to
be considerate.

I expect my health
to remain excellent
until I'm very old.

I expect you to
stop making those
faces at me.

How's that battle
with reality working
out for you?

There are two types of expectations: the expectations we have on the outside world and the expectations the outside world has on us. Because we have to make an interpretation of what the outside world is expecting of us, both types are actually internal and can be changed by us.

Expecting the world to treat you as you believe you should be treated is not realistic. If you expect people to keep their word, behave morally, treat you kindly because of your generosity, or treat you with gratitude for your present or past gifts, you will fail. Claiming to know how others will behave in the future is to "know it all" and also to know the future. Both are impossible. In fact, expectations are not real. They are completely inside your head.

Instead, notice but don't stay attached to your expectations. Realize that expectations do not match reality. Acknowledge that the future is unknowable. As you let go of expectations, you will be learning to accept reality as it is. Giving up demands on reality will lead to your freedom.

Expectations are quickly followed by judgments. When an expectation is not met, we are quick to condemn. Judgments separate us from reality, from others, and from ourselves. (More is written about judgments in Chapters Four and Seven.)

Having zero expectations does not mean we cannot have goals, nor does it prevent our speculating about the future. Also, there is a difference between expectations and faith. Unlike expectations, faith has no form. When we make demands about what forms our specific desires must take, we are becoming trapped by expectations. (More is written about faith in Chapters Six, Seven, and Ten.)

THE PAST IS GONE

If you are present, you can give up all expectations.

Acceptance and Commitment Therapy (ACT) teaches the concept to "take your storyline lightly." This is excellent advice for anyone who remains attached to the benefits of expectations. If you are not too full of the importance of your own story, then you do not have to hold on to your expectations. Letting go of your own self-importance frees you from having to seek the approval of a world that seems to demand that you be a certain way.

I don't have a problem
with expectations.

I expect everyone
to do the unexpected.

I didn't
expect that!

Being fully in the moment brings you to the place where there are no expectations. People feel calm when they deeply concentrate on a task or meditate on the spiritual. Calmness replaces expectations when you are intensely focused and mindful of the present.

Only by having zero expectations will the past be gone. Only by having zero expectations can you stop the future from hurting you. Only by having zero expectations can you be free from failure. Only by having zero expectations can you live in The Now. Only by having zero expectations will every moment be an eternity of reverence, gratitude, and a heart open to receive Grace. Living without expectations is Living Yes.

EXPECTATIONS AND GOALS

Expectations are not goals.

What is an expectation? An expectation is a specific demand about the present based on preset beliefs about the past. What is a goal? A goal is guidance about actions that we hope will improve the future. Giving up expectations does not mean giving up the energy to pursue your future. Expectations are not required in order to have goals. Expectations are not required in order to have hopes. Expectations are not required in order to have dreams.

Expectations are different from goals, ambitions, hopes, or dreams. With expectations, your demands are either met or not met. Outcome is either attained or not. On the other hand, goals and ambitions are targets. Whether you hit or miss the target provides information that helps you guide your aim the next time. A goal is a target that gives your ambition direction.

Consider yourself an archer with a bow and arrow. You set the goal to hit the bull's-eye and have the intent to hit it. Aiming for the center of the target is an action to meet that goal. Having to hit the target every time is an expectation, which will probably not be met. If you expect to hit the bull's-eye every time, you will fail and feel frustrated. When you come back the next day, still expecting to do well, you may face anxiety as you draw the bow back. When you miss, you will quickly return to frustration and anger, probably even more quickly than you did the day before. Your anxiety will grow. As you keep missing, your anger will grow in an endless cycle until you begin to expect failure. You may become unmotivated, sad, and lose hope.

If you lower your expectations, you can reduce your anger and anxiety and raise your satisfaction level, but if you have zero expectations, failure will have no effect on you. You can continue to do the best you can, concentrate more clearly in the moment, and work to get closer to your goal. Without frustration or anxiety to set back your self-confidence, you are more likely to improve your skills more rapidly and face failure less often. Eliminate your expectations while you continue to maintain your goals and ambitions. You will feel less frustration and more peace.

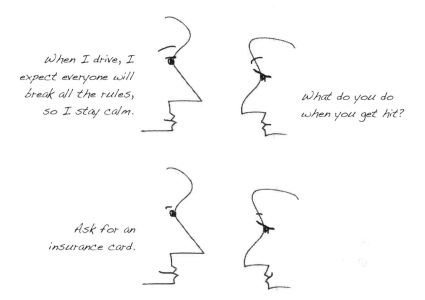

When I drive, I expect everyone will break all the rules, so I stay calm.

What do you do when you get hit?

Ask for an insurance card.

EXPECTATIONS AND SPECULATION ABOUT THE FUTURE

Expectations block you from future possibilities.

Gambling is speculation about the future. We consider the possibility that we have a chance of winning, so we play the odds. We are hoping our calculations will result in a payoff. We know there is a chance we may lose. We are not expecting to win.

We speculate or evaluate in all areas of our lives, such as finding our mates, quitting our job and going to school, putting our money in a bank, or pushing the gas pedal to enter traffic when the light turns green. All these speculations about the future call on us to make our best calculations in the moment. Through all of them, the future is unknowable.

If you don't like what happens as a result of your choices, your demanding expectations set you up to react with an unpleasant emotion. However, as long as you are not attached to the outcome, then you are not holding demanding expectations.

Intelligent speculation can be done calmly at any risk level. But you are wise to be careful. If you enjoy the rush, you may go back just for the thrill. If you go for the thrill too much, you may make destructive choices and may have a gambling problem. At that point, your expectations are way out of whack!

If you stay open to the possibility that you may not always correctly predict what will happen, and you realize that you may not get others to behave the way you demand that they do, then you will remain clear-thinking and quickly return to balance.

EXERCISE — TWENTY-TWO WAYS TO PLAY AT LIVING YES ☒

Sometimes you can improve your mood by doing things. Psychologists call this "behavioral activation." You can activate yourself by behaving in ways that connect you to your world. There are many areas where you can improve your health and a lot has been written about them. Take care of yourself physically, exercise and stretch your body, stay away from drugs and alcohol. Eat smart, use medical services when needed, be willing to seek help.

But if you're willing to play, there's more. Here are twenty-two solid and creative ideas for Living Yes. Pick some that seem hard and be sure to choose the ones that line up with what you value.

CREATIVE IDEAS FOR LIVING YES
1. Change your appearance. Wear a funny hat, a bright shirt. Streak your hair. Grow a mustache or paste one on.
2. Enjoy a meal. Eat in silence. Don't put more food in your mouth until you've completely chewed the previous bite.
3. Drink more water than you can imagine drinking.

CREATIVE IDEAS FOR LIVING YES (CONT.)

4. Look at the night sky. Figure out the moon phase. Learn to tell a star from a planet. Find the moon or a planet during the daytime.

5. Go into the woods. Visit a museum, a garden, or a dog park.

6. Telephone someone who would be surprised to hear from you. Maybe call someone you liked from the distant past or an acquaintance you barely know.

7. Go out with your spouse and another couple.

8. Play a board game with friends – Pictionary and Loaded Questions are two good community games.

9. Read some history, or research your ancestors.

10. Take a nap. Sleep enough hours. Get up very early when you don't have to.

11. Give some of your stuff away. Charity job programs seek dress clothes, decent shoes, and used eyeglasses.

12. Switch between being more childlike and less childlike.

13. Learn to listen. You don't have to be heard. Go on lengthy talk-fasts, not saying a word for an entire day. On the other hand, if you're shy, talk and speak out.

14. Sing.

15. Dance.

16. Create objects and give them away.

17. Do something you're not skilled at, such as yoga, baseball, singing, dancing, painting, learning another language. Allow yourself to stumble, and accept your joy and effort as enough.

CREATIVE IDEAS FOR LIVING YES (CONT.)
18. Go out when you feel listless. Go home when you are fulfilled or you've done enough.
19. Help someone.
20. Pray without begging. Talk to God in the language of your heart.
21. Meditate. Find the silence.
22. Make a list of twenty-two more ways to Live Yes.

PROGRESS CHECK

Do you know where you fake it in your life?

What false ideas could you give up to live your life with zero expectations?

How are you trapped by your thinking about the past or your worrying about the future?

What fun ways did you find to play at Living Yes?

Learning Acceptance

BEING RIGHT

You have the right to remain willing.

The "know it all" problem goes beyond expectations. When we think we know what is right, we are likely to be wrong. We are probably stuck thinking "my way or the highway." When we think we know the way instead of waiting for Life to unfold, it is wise for us to examine how we are being selfish. Some call this "king baby" behavior. King baby is the immature *enfant terrible* in us who is not open, is stuck in his beliefs, and certainly not teachable. (Of course, "queen baby" has the same problem.) Granted, sometimes it is necessary to stand for principle and set proper boundaries, but if our way to resist is to puff ourselves up, to become rigid, a healthier choice is to remain mentally flexible.

People confuse being right with demanding that they deserve their rights. Living Yes means that we no longer have to prove we are right. Instead we can accept Life just as it is without the personal responsibility to control everything or fix anything. Abilities are not the same as rights.

Our first responsibility to Live Yes is to step out of prearranged traps of how we believe we're supposed to think. Living Yes means we choose to be human and limited rather than forcing our thinking on others. We can step out of preset fate and follow our unique destiny of Living Yes. (More is written about destiny in Chapter Eight.)

When you admit that you are not entitled to being right, you find peace. The only rights you have are the rights bestowed by Reality, and you cannot know for sure what those may be. Man-made rights are temporary. If you give up demanding all of your man-made rights, you will have the chance to be willing and free.

This works much like expectations. Zero expectations. Zero demand for our so-called "rights." Radical acceptance. Full openness to what is.

ACCEPTANCE IS THE ANSWER

Acceptance is not the same as giving in.

Sometimes we give in to situations too easily in the name of "acceptance." Instead of admitting that we are trapped in No, we back down to relieve our discomfort. The problems go away only until the next time we're pushed. We are choosing to admit our self-doubts and what we see as our weakness. We have used the noble idea of acceptance to actually practice avoidance. As we will learn in the next chapter, boundaries give us a chance to act and Live Yes.

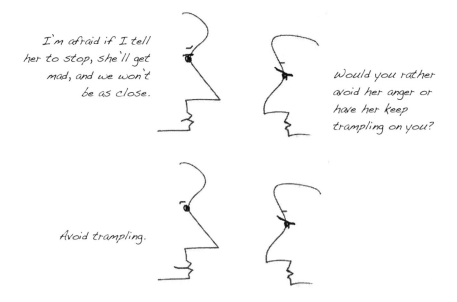

There is an old rule in writing stories that action is character. We don't know a person by what he says. We know him by what he does. Uncle Joey may say he hates smoking and he's going to quit, but because he keeps picking up cigarettes every day for fifty-five years, we realize Uncle Joey is committed to continuing to smoke. If Uncle Joey accepted the hazards of smoking and wished to avoid them, he wouldn't pick up another cigarette again. The very act of acceptance brings change.

ACCEPTING LIFE ON LIFE'S TERMS, EVEN WHEN IT'S HARD

Sometimes acceptance means learning how to be uncomfortable.

There are ways to change our behavior—eating, sleeping, exercising, smoking, drinking. And there are ways to improve our ability to get along with others, achieve our goals, and "win friends and influence people" (as Dale Carnegie helped us do in 1937).

My friend Helena is a playful person. She finds acceptance in two words, each pronounced thickly in her ancestral Cuban accent: "whatteber" and "jounehbanoh." When something happens that she does not like and cannot control, she just says "whatteber." When she is about to worry about something that may or may not happen, she says "jounehbanoh." In case you haven't made the translation yet, when she says "whatteber," she is accepting her own limits with "whatever," and when she says "jounehbanoh," she is recognizing that she cannot predict the future with "you never know."

We can accept Reality by learning our own ways to soothe ourselves in healthful ways during painful times. We can choose willingness rather than willfulness. We can do what's needed instead of resisting or indulging. We can let go of what is supposed to be "right," take a "time-out," distract ourselves, access our breath, walk, listen to music, bathe, have a warm

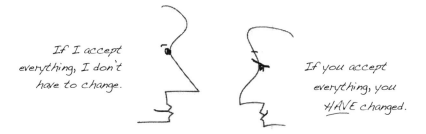

If I accept everything, I don't have to change.

If you accept everything, you HAVE changed.

drink, do something nice for someone, or meditate. These acceptance strategies are ways to Live Yes.

As one of my students says, "If you don't learn to accept your ups and downs, you'll always be down." Be human, not all-powerful. Know we are limited. He adds, "We build ourselves up so much that we think we don't have problems. I'm no longer superman, and I can't fix everything. Now I stay away from kryptonite. I have learned I don't have to figure things out. I can't change it. Life offers me more than to become stuck in one spot." He has learned to not let his mind rule over him, and the result is that he feels deeply connected to Life itself.

Demands can be unnecessary. Demands can be unrealistic and unreasonable. Demands can be relentless and uncontrollable. Demands do not include freedom to choose. Without choice, we cannot find acceptance. When we demand change or refuse to accept ourselves or others, we are clearly trapped in a rigid No. Let's give up those demands, so we can Live Yes.

Do the following acceptance process with an open heart. No "buts," no regrets, no resentment. Let it go.

EXERCISE: THE ACCEPTANCE PROCESS

1. Re-experience the specific event that you are frustrated (saddened or ashamed) about. Put the event into a very short trigger phrase (such as "I saw the letter," "My weight on the scale was 233 pounds," or "She said, 'Get out!'").

2. Say out loud the trigger phrase and the answer phrase, over and over again: "It happened. I can accept it".

3. You may change to other answer phrases, but always stay with the same trigger phrase.

Here are some script examples:

Say the trigger phrase then say:
"It happened. I can accept it."

Say the trigger phrase again, and then say:
"It happened. I don't like it."

Say the trigger phrase again, and then say:
"It happened. I can accept it."

Say the trigger phrase again, and then say:
"It happened. I may accept it.

Say the trigger phrase again, and then say:
"It happened. I can accept it."

Say the trigger phrase again, and then say:
"It happened. I can't control the universe."

Say the trigger phrase again, and then say:
"It happened. I am accepting it."

Say the trigger phrase again, and then say:
"It happened. My expectations are not real."

Say the trigger phrase again, and then say:
"It happened. I do accept it."

Keep repeating until you accept it. Then if you want to
Live Yes even more deeply, go to the next part.

4. Add gratitude for the event. (We call this a "Hot Yes.")
Say the trigger phrase again, and then say:
"It happened. I can embrace it!

Say the trigger phrase again, and then say:
"It happened. I can be grateful for it."

Say the trigger phrase again, and then say:
"It happened. I can embrace it!"

Say the trigger phrase again, and then say:
"It happened. I am grateful for it!"

Say the trigger phrase again, and then say:
"It happened. I can embrace it."

Say the trigger phrase again, and then say:
"It happened. I can be grateful for it!"

Say the trigger phrase again, and then say:
"It happened. It is a spiritual gift."

Say the trigger phrase again, and then say:
"It happened. I am embracing it!"

Keep repeating until you can fully accept it. (More is written
about Hot Yes at the end of this chapter.)

ACCEPTANCE AND SPIRIT

Acceptance opens you to spirit.

Living Yes means accepting our highest self. Living Yes means we realize we are part of one Source. The goal is to be "happy, joyous, and free." Total acceptance is a very peaceful place.

The way we see the world sets up the way we are going to respond to it. I once saw on a blackboard, "People don't C the world as it is. They C the world as they R." So true. Changes in action are changes in character. Changes in character result in new life experiences. As one client put it, "I can change from what I was to what I am." Living Yes brings deep acceptance that creates change.

When we think about someone we're annoyed with, we feel heavier, and when we think about someone who's easy to love, we feel lighter. We may notice that when we believe our lies, we feel heavier; and when we believe our truths, we feel lighter. Becoming aware of the weight in our body will help us to make choices that will lighten our load. Acceptance may be surprising and seem like magic. We are happiest (fulfilled and centered) when we go beyond reason, sense, and feeling. Attuning with body and mind for signals of our limits, we find All Is Well.

Acceptance is not the same as surrender. Our inner soldier may want to fight instead of surrender. Yet, being rigid and refusing to retreat may be the trap that gets us surrounded. If we can resist our limited, reactive ego-mind, which is blocking out a higher truth, we can allow ourselves to Live Yes with full and radical acceptance.

As you drive the winding highway of your life, you are going to run into obstacles. When something gets in your way, you can respond with Yes or No. Or you can say "No!" to No, slam on the brakes, and avoid hitting the tree or the problem altogether. Saying "No" to No is an effective way to Live Yes. However, you can Live Yes another way. You can change your direction, steer away from the problem, and step on the gas in a new and healthful direction.

DYNAMICALLY LIVING YES

There is not a Yes-or-No answer. Life doesn't stand still.
Living Yes is an ongoing challenge and opportunity.

Dynamic means moving. Life is always on the move. In fact, it moves wherever we least expect it (remember expectations?). Life is an ongoing, lesson-giving machine. Walter Cole was quoted as saying, "We must look for the opportunity in every difficulty instead of being paralyzed at the thought of the difficulty in every opportunity." That is the nature of Living Yes. Life constantly brings fresh challenges that invite us to reinvent ourselves every moment of every day. The question is, what are we going to do about it?

When the world brings us what we do not expect, we may choose to be flexible or rigid. If we are stuck thinking "that's who I am" then we will be hit across the face with a smack from Life. By staying clear of our limited view of who we are or how we believe the world must work, we may choose to be physically healthy, mentally clear, and emotionally flexible.

We can solve this from two sides. Experts say we need to learn (1) "desensitization" and (2) "stress inoculation." In other words, we can learn (1) to not take things too personally, to not be over-sensitive, and (2) we can also learn to handle our discomfort and not be over-reactive. Both are part of the path to Live Yes.

Sometimes the painful experiences teach us healthful ways

to deal with problems, but when the problems are removed, we don't change our defenses. We hold on to a mistaken idea of who we are that prevents us from staying mentally and emotionally flexible. The result is anger, confusion, sadness, and pain. Changing is difficult for some. For others it's easy. For all, it is a measure of our ability to adapt and remain balanced.

If we Live Yes, we respond to our life as it changes without becoming stuck in a rigid idea of who we are and how we are supposed to behave. Instead, we discover the openness of each moment. We learn how to identify our habits consciously, so we may be able to continue to see which behaviors are constructive and which are destructive. That is how to live dynamically. When you make a choice to live openly with whatever may come, you are equipped to embrace each moment fully and experience All that is offered.

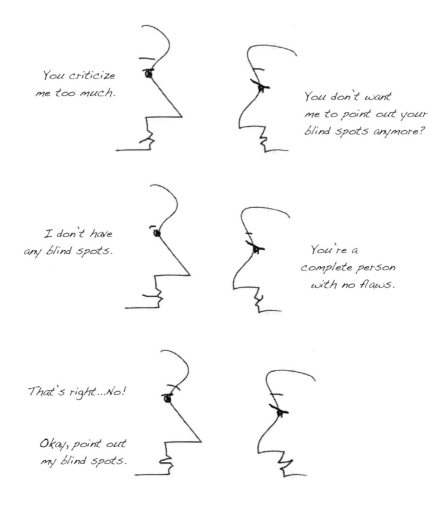

We do not like to discover our own denial and rigidness. It is hard to learn how to Live Yes with acceptance and flexibility. Yet it is the only way. Once you know your direction, you may set a course that will help you create a vision of what you want. This is called "Values Centered Direction," and the Opposite Values Process is one way to get a clue about yours.

EXERCISE – THE OPPOSITE VALUES PROCESS

To create a vision of what you want:

1. Select a troubling incident or area of your life.

2. In the first column, write everything you don't like about the situation, all the complaints, criticisms, negative attitudes. Be sure to include problems about yourself, others, and the situation (context).

3. In the second column, list the opposite, ideal quality.

4. Picture (envision) a world described in the second column. Reflect on what you could do to create it. As you move through life, stay flexible, especially about making choices to move toward your vision.

Example: My Job

DON'T LIKE	IDEAL
Boring	Exciting
Punch Clock	Flexible hours
Limited authority	Able to run things as I wish
Difficult clients	Grateful and supportive clients
Not smart enough	Smart, confident, capable, respected

Creative Visualization helps your unconscious mind create your vision. By specifically picturing what you want to create (without demands or expectations), the process automatically begins. These mental rehearsals prepare you to create yourself as the person you choose to be. Start by creatively visualizing how you can move from No to Yes with the model on the next page.

By now you may realize that Living Yes is a simple yet difficult choice. You are either set in your reactions and fighting what is happening (stuck in No) or you are moving with the comings and goings of your experiences (Living Yes). Living Yes is an approach to life that calls you to face your fears. You can work your way up from bondage to freedom if you are willing to keep doing your best over and over.

The movement up and down from No to Yes and back is an ongoing process, which can be seen in four stages: 1. Hot No; 2. Cool No; 3. Cool Yes; and 4. Hot Yes. A situation (Life trigger) occurs, and you respond at any one of the four stages. Since your life is always changing, you are offered repeated opportunities to respond. As you gain clarity and apply courage, you may work yourself up the ladder to Live Yes. You can also get stuck in No, such as holding on to your expectations, and slide deeper into the pit.

FOUR STAGES OF MOVING FROM NO TO YES

STAGE 1: HOT NO

Resigning, giving up, fighting, rebelling, opposing, rejecting, making the event wrong. Addiction. Willfulness. There is no way out. Stuck because you think you are fighting for survival. Result is painful, separating emotion (anger, fear, sadness, confusion).

STAGE 2: COOL NO

Reasoning but still No, putting up with it, getting by, avoiding, justifying, habitual behavior, using your thinking skills to endure and disconnect. Obligation. Having to prove yourself. Exerting self-control. Cooling the inner heat.

STAGE 3: COOL YES

Accepting, coping, letting it be, letting go of demanding expectations and unhealthful judgments, getting that it's okay, becoming conscious, surrendering, discovering moments of connecting emotions: happiness and peace.

STAGE 4: HOT YES

Embracing it, choosing it, gathering your power and trusting yourself, living into it, being fully present, feeling whatever you feel, looking beyond self, noble sacrifice, seeing growth opportunities, open to undreamed-of possibilities, zero demands, zero expectations, trusting that it's best this way, allowing it to give you energy and growth, serenity.

PROGRESS CHECK

How do you get trapped being "right?"

Can you identify a time when you wanted to stay "comfortable," even when you knew it wasn't the best choice for you?

Did you do the Acceptance Process out loud? What happened for you?

Using the Opposites columns, can you identify your deepest personal values?

Write an example from your own life of each of the four stages of moving from No to Yes (Hot No, Cool No, Cool Yes, Hot Yes).

3   Setting Boundaries and Sticking with Them

COST/BENEFIT OF SETTING BOUNDARIES

You can be nice and say "No." The result will be respect.

Let's start by comparing disadvantages to advantages. Not setting boundaries with others costs us in ways that we know very well: being abused, being run over, exposing our weakness, expressing our helplessness, always being the victim. Allowing ourselves to be a doormat may seem easier at the time, but getting by and giving in doesn't do us much good down the road. The cost of not setting boundaries is painful in the long term.

On the benefits side, setting healthy boundaries with others protects us from losing ourselves at the expense of others' demands. Strong boundaries allow us to stand on a foundation of strength, self-love and self-confidence. Healthy boundaries are the key to maintaining our inner worth, our self-control, and our self-respect. Boundaries preserve our ability to remain clear about our individual identity. With boundaries, we are able to be fully adult and take care of ourselves.

Clear boundaries allow us to communicate with others as partners. They help us to take responsibility to be loving. No one can have a healthful relationship without clear boundaries. They are required for direct and honest communication. Setting clear boundaries results in a deeper and more genuine connection with others. Boundaries enable us to maintain our freedom and to exercise our freedom rights. Boundaries position us to practice being clear and assertive.

Healthy boundaries provide physical and emotional

protection. They distinguish our individual selves from the entire society. The old saying "Good fences make good neighbors" means that good boundaries lead to strong and safe relationships. By setting clear boundaries, we avoid stepping into a hornets' nest of confusion, rage, and possible despair. Setting boundaries demonstrates our ability to stand in our personal power. Boundaries help us combat being violated and falling into the victim role. With effective boundaries we may be our true selves.

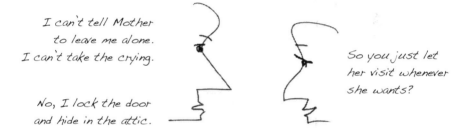

I can't tell Mother to leave me alone. I can't take the crying.

No, I lock the door and hide in the attic.

So you just let her visit whenever she wants?

Healthy boundaries are not walls. They are changeable. Like our skin, they keep out infections, but let in the energy from sunlight. Boundaries may vary with context. For example, you behave differently when the kids are around. When they're not, the boundaries shift appropriately.

To maintain these benefits, create clear, safe boundaries with enforceable consequences by using the following three-step model.

Special note: Living Yes means living safe and smart. Some relationships are dangerous. Please do not take these ideas and put yourself in a situation that will risk your safety. Instead, if you are in any danger, seek professional therapeutic and law enforcement help.

EXERCISE — THE THREE-STEP MODEL FOR
SETTING BOUNDARIES   ⊠

1. Plan

2. Assert and Be Heard

3. Implement Consequences

Here's how to do the three steps.

1. Plan: Decide what you will and will not accept. (This may take some thinking.) Then, for each possibility you can imagine, decide consequences. As the behaviors get worse, increase the consequences. (Consider writing this plan in a notebook.)

Example of Planning. Realize that being yelled at for having dinner late is unacceptable, and you won't take it anymore. Decide that if you are yelled at, you will leave the house and stay with your sister.

2. Assert and Be Heard: Express your boundary. Then (if necessary) state the first consequences that you will use if your boundaries are violated. State only those consequences that you are willing to do. Consequences are not a threat; they are promised action. Finally, confirm you've been heard. The best way is hearing your exact words said back to you.

Example of Assert and Be Heard. State the simple truth to your abuser: "Yelling at me is unacceptable, and I will leave if you yell at me again." Be sure to hear back the words, such as "I understand that if I yell at you again, you say you will leave."

3. Consequences: If your boundaries are crossed, implement consequences. If you don't, you become a victim and will certainly be violated again.

Example of Consequences. If yelled at, leave the house, and work the three steps again.

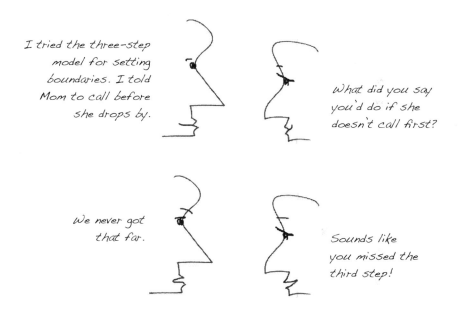

I tried the three-step model for setting boundaries. I told Mom to call before she drops by.

What did you say you'd do if she doesn't call first?

We never got that far.

Sounds like you missed the third step!

BEING ASSERTIVE

Assertive behavior is honest and clear.

Clear boundary-setting is neither a threat nor an effort to control someone else. By setting a boundary, we are communicating a cause-effect response if our needs are not met. Our freedom does not come from others' behavior. Our freedom comes from our standing up for ourselves with our own boundaries. This is true even if they violate them again. But this time, if they act out, we are no longer willing to be the victim.

As we assert our boundaries, we may remain at peace by holding zero expectations of what will happen.

Assertiveness is not the same as being aggressive, passive, or passive-aggressive. Assertiveness is stating your intentions clearly without manipulating or raising your voice. Aggressiveness is using anger to force your way. Passiveness is refusing to assert anything. Passive-aggressive is being aggressive while appearing passive. Passive-aggression is the often-annoying behavior of being too cool about a given situation.

The chart on the next page illustrates some of the characteristics of each.

Here is some matter-of-fact language that can help you assert your boundaries.

"Please do not swear at me, or I will leave the room."

"I am not going to stay here if you keep yelling at me."

"I become very uncomfortable when you drink too much. Will that be your last drink? If not, I will leave the restaurant."

"I refuse to play the victim. If you continue to insult me, I will demand that you leave."

OVERCOMING RESISTANCE TO SETTING BOUNDARIES
Weakness is not the same as niceness.

You always have the option to end your relationship with any person, even family members. Choosing to stay in a bad relationship is a passive, get-along-at-any-cost decision, which is based on fear rather than on your worth and strength.

Resentment of self or others has no benefit. Blaming doesn't do you any good. If you are seeking approval from

Aggressive, Passive, Passive-Aggressive, Assertive Behaviors

AGGRESSIVE	PASSIVE	PASSIVE-AGGRESSIVE	ASSERTIVE
Loud	Soft	Quiet	Calm
Interrupts	Afraid to speak	Doesn't speak	Open
Confronts	Avoids	Avoids	Relaxed
Rigid	Rigid	Rigid	Flexible
Intimidates	Isolates	Isolates	Engages
Controlling	Goes along	Appears to go along	To the point
Stares	Avoids looking	May stare but will look away	Good eye contact
Values self more than others	Values self less than others	Values self more than others until pressed	Values self equal to others
I'm okay; you're not.	You're okay; I'm not.	I'm okay, you're not, but I pretend you're okay and I'm not.	I'm okay; you're okay.
Has to put others down to protect self.	Never makes anyone uncomfortable or displeases anyone except self.	Must not hold painful feelings. Must be comfortable.	Responsible to protect my own rights.
NO	NO	NO	YES

the relationship, you have lost your power and are choosing to be a victim. Setting boundaries is the way to reverse this downward cycle.

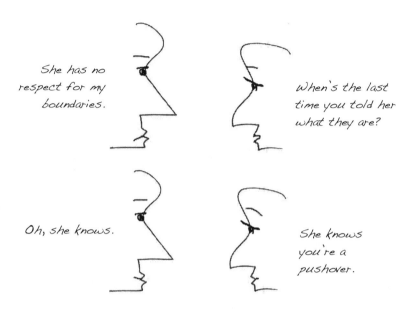

Communicate what you want directly. There will be no need to enforce consequences if you are clear enough *and* the person is willing to respect your needs.

A misguided desire to prove or survive at any cost will not work. You do not have to do anything. You are making a choice.

Efforts to be likable can put you in a position of pretending. If you pretend, others will notice that you are easily manipulated, and will take advantage of you. If you are honest and set boundaries, they will not challenge you, and they will mask their weakness by picking on someone else until they learn to Live Yes. Likability comes from being real, not from being passive.

If you abandon yourself and join with another person, you will not automatically become stronger. Don't believe this myth. Some will give themselves over to another in a desperate demand to get support. Others will prop themselves up by picking a partner who is needy. Strong individuals make the best partners, and when you are already strong, you make the best partner.

Those who are abusing you are probably covering their own weakness with a show of false strength. Jealousy, power grabs, fake superiority are all games that have to be taken seriously, but you don't have to buy in to them. Even if your weak position makes partnering seem logical, it's frightening because you're entering a house of cards.

There is no advantage in proving yourself to someone else if you compromise your values. You are not obligated to anyone unless you choose to be. Do not be a victim of your own fear.

Living up to your boundaries within your values is a necessary practice. Set boundaries that allow you to be who you really are.

Focus on your mutual needs, not on each other's flaws and weaknesses. You're not perfect, and they're not perfect. Leave enough wiggle room but not enough to compromise your values.

It is not your responsibility to take care of someone else's feelings, even children. Especially children.

It is not healthful to break boundaries to protect others from their own discomfort or feelings.

Setting clear boundaries may require you to tolerate others directing their anger, hurt, fear, tears, even yelling toward you. (Tools that will help you learn to use your humanity and strength will be provided in Chapters Five and Six.) Sometimes you will have to tap into your deepest values in order to maintain clear boundaries. (More is written about values in Chapter Eight.)

After setting boundaries or enforcing consequences, you may accuse yourself of being weak, guilty, ashamed, unlovable, or worthless. Those unnecessary thoughts come from your childhood and are the opposite of your present actions, which are strong, clear, and self-actualized.

You are likely to be challenged and tested, and you may be surprised by others' respect and compliance.

View the person's behavior from a sensible outsider's perspective.

You are more likely to create a "win-win" situation if you avoid being angry or personal.

Sometimes avoidance shows your weakness around others. On the other hand, sometimes you may be assertive and then step away from emotional danger. This is not avoidance; it is self-protection.

Boundary setting is not mastered in one event. It is an ongoing process. Start small and learn the skill. When you trust yourself, setting boundaries will be satisfying and empowering.

A strong support system is helpful. Have someone around who helps you keep your word and cares about you. Having someone there will help you hold your high self-esteem. (More is written about support in Chapter Eight.)

Even when we are skilled at being assertive and setting clear boundaries, conflict does not stop. Sometimes we feel uncomfortable and avoid conflict. This makes our lives more difficult in the long run. But conflict can be valuable. It leads to growth, like a muscle breaking down in exercise in order to grow back stronger. If we had no conflict, we would have no reason to set boundaries or be assertive.

Stories throughout the ages, including popular movies and TV shows, depend on conflict to keep them moving. There are three types of conflict: external conflict (climbing a mountain or not having enough money to buy groceries); internal conflict (struggles inside our head, such as ethical challenges); and relational conflict (oppositions with others and competing interests). Conflict is a motivator, a challenge that helps us move forward. Accepting this is to Live Yes.

ASSERT YOUR RIGHTS

I have the right to keep my thoughts to myself.

I have the right to keep my feelings to myself.

I have the right to keep what I do to myself.

I have the right to keep my business to myself.

I have the right to keep my beliefs to myself.

I have the right to express myself and protect myself.

I don't have to be nice to others.

I don't have to be logical.

I don't deserve to be abused or disrespected. I am not a victim. I do not have to let anyone take advantage of me.

I have the right to love, respect, and to protect myself.

I have the right to say, "I don't understand."

What others think of me is none of my business.

I don't have to live as others have told me or trained me, and I do not have to feel guilty when I stand up to those ideas or people who present them to me.

I have the right to self-acceptance.

I have the right to love and respect.

CONTROL ROLES

Don't be a persecutor, victim, or rescuer.

Communicating boundaries does not work in all situations. For example, if someone is in a screaming rage or too drunk, it's not a good time to confront them. Instead, protect yourself by getting out of danger. It is not your responsibility to punish them, play the victim, or rescue them. Instead, do what is best for you and them in the long run.

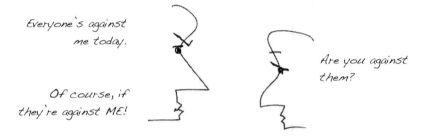

There is a behavior pattern called the "Karpman drama triangle" which looks like this:

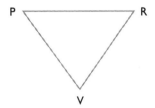

P is "persecutor," V is "victim," and R is "rescuer." A persecutor is someone who aims to injure another. Persecutor behavior results from resentment. A victim is someone who believes they are being persecuted. Victim behavior results from self-pity. A rescuer is someone who wants to protect the victim from the persecutor and sees herself as a savior. Rescuer behavior results from self-righteousness. All those behaviors potentially trap us.

To break free, do not join with those who are in the other roles. You can't persecute if there's no one to attack. You can't be a victim if you don't react to an attack. You can't rescue if there's no victim. While it is sometimes necessary to set a moral boundary or choose assertive behavior, those who play persecutor, victim, or rescuer have taken those behaviors to extremes, selling out their own best interests.

Persecutors say "No" by blaming, criticizing, indulging anger, setting overly strict limits, working to control, and being overly severe.

Victims say "No" by holding themselves helpless, hopeless, powerless, ashamed, seeking rescuers instead of taking responsibility, not facing painful truths, and avoiding making choices.

Rescuers are sometimes called enablers. They step in where they are not wanted. They manipulate others and often use guilt to keep victims dependent. They refuse to let others fail. Like victims, they are too soft to set boundaries. They have not yet learned that if you show too much mercy, you create victims.

Those strategies are attempts to control what cannot be controlled. The persecutor and rescuer make efforts to control the victim while the victim lets others control them. None are taking responsibility for themselves.

Someone may become a persecutor because he believes his righteousness is above others and victims deserve their punishment. Someone may become a victim by not setting boundaries and standing up for themselves. Someone may become a rescuer by sacrificing themselves for others to the point that both end up drowning. (This is called "co-dependence.") Those behaviors are usually unconscious. Becoming aware of this behavior is the first step.

Living Yes begins by discovering how much you are contributing to getting stuck in the P – V – R triangle. If you are playing persecutor, victim, or rescuer, take steps to get out of the trap. Seek equality and balance in relationships. Treat everyone with respect. Set and follow-through with healthy boundaries. Walk away when necessary. Get away from those who are taking advantage of you. By taking care of your Self, you will be on a path to Live Yes.

PROGRESS CHECK

Can you think of someone with whom you are going to set a clear boundary?

Can you pick situations when you were aggressive, passive, passive-aggressive, and assertive?

What are the problems you have with setting boundaries, and how are you going to set boundaries anyway?

Can you see a situation where you played victim? Was there a persecutor or rescuer?

Can you see a time when you played persecutor or rescuer?

Who filled in the other roles?

4 The Voice in Your Head

THE TWO VOICES

The little chatterbox in your head is a big liar.

Inside of your head is a constant, talking voice. Triggered by events, physical sensations, and what others say to you, your head is filled with an unstoppable flow of mind chatter. The more you resist the chatter, the louder and more real it sounds. This voice in your head has been given names like "self-talk," "automatic thinking," "inner dialogue," and "the reactive mind."

EXERCISE—WRITING THE SELF-TALK

This is the only time I will invite you to go all out "No!" Be assured, the rest of the chapter will help you discover how to Live Yes.

1. Take out some paper (it's even better than typing on a computer) and describe something specific that's bugging you. Below that write everything your mind is saying about the situation. Include the harshest judgments. Write how others should behave. Rant about how someone is annoying you. Complain about anything or anyone. You don't have to be nice. You don't have to be mature. You don't have to be logical. You may even contradict yourself. Admit what scares you. Admit what makes you sad. Predict the future. Demand changes in others. Give advice to everyone. If you haven't done so already, turn inward and attack yourself with the same judgments, rants, fears, complaints, and demands. Keep going until you can't think of one more thought. If more thoughts come later, return to the paper and write them.

2. Notice how you feel as you write all those nasty thoughts. You may feel relief at having the opportunity to slow down and express the thoughts on paper, or you may feel deepening anger, sadness, and anxiety. Whatever you may feel, observe how the thoughts are causing the feelings.

3. Now set the paper aside, and do something nice for yourself. Come back to this list after you've mastered some of the Living Yes techniques in the next four chapters. It will help you see how much you've learned.

~~~~~~

You may be noticing that your head is filled with a constant flow of words that are crowded with lies – not accurate, not complete, and not balanced. Those unstoppable sentences about everything sound like your own voice. The mind is filled with expectations of yourself and others. The mind makes false judgments about how bad things are: "If I spill that drink on my shirt, I'll be a slob and everyone will think I'm a slob." The mind makes faulty assumptions: "If I call in sick, they'll fire me." It catastrophizes: "I'm going to freeze to death in this weather." It gets stuck in rigid viewpoints: "When he insults me, I can't be nice to him." It judges without compassion or forgiveness: "She should be nicer to her mom." It makes unfair demands: "If I don't get that promotion, I'll have to quit." It pretends to know the answer: "I'm not pretty enough to keep a husband." It does all those at once: "If I don't understand every part of this book, I'm doomed." All the noise blocks you from Living Yes.

Here's the key: *Most of this self-talk is a lie.* That's right. The voice in your head is a big liar (like delusion in eastern religion or the devil in the Bible and Quran). And even worse, when you believe those lies, you feel sad, annoyed, anxious, and miserable.

The chatter between your ears is as old as Genesis. In the Garden of Eden the crafty snake does everything in his power to tempt Eve to eat the apple. He gets inside her head with sneaky ideas: "God didn't tell you; he told the man." "What is God hiding from you? You'll know good from evil." "You know it's true." "You'll have the power." "You won't die." Still today, all those ideas represent the reactive mind as it tries to lead you along the path away from Living Yes.

The remarkable idea is: Your thoughts are not the same as who you are! They are visitors in your home, but you are the owner. Those thoughts can be lousy guests who will lead you on the path away from Living Yes. Understanding where they come from and how they lie is the key to self-improvement. Learning to hear the self-talk is the first step. Challenging the self-talk is the way you begin to Live Yes. More awareness will result in more awareness.

While all this destructive reacting is going on in your head, you can begin to slow the chatter by calling it what it is and demanding that it STOP! Make the first efforts to notice the flow and STOP IT. Maybe you can think of a stop image like holding up a big red stop sign or pulling a bathtub plug. Once you stop the flow, it will be easier to step back and find helpful thoughts. In the next few chapters, we will look at some specific tools you can use to do this, but willing it to STOP is excellent training

I get annoyed when my neighbor plays his music all night long.

I just want it to stop.

Do you want to keep thinking about it or do you want to let go of your anger?

and will prepare you for the next steps.

When we get excited or annoyed, we tend to talk too much (or too little). We become overly defensive. We let our racing thoughts drive our judgment, and we blurt out whatever reactive thought comes into our heads. It's helpful to learn to slow the thinking, so we may act smarter. Can you imagine what it would be like if the self-talk completely stopped? What would your life be like if you didn't care what has already happened and didn't worry about tomorrow? What would your life be like if you responded with a quiet mind? Would you gain deep awareness of the moment? Would you be able to be the essential you? How would you face changes if your head were quiet and content?

We will begin by unpacking the lies. Later you will learn more about how to practice stepping back from the self-talk into the so-called "seat of the soul," a goal that spiritual masters of east and west have sought for centuries.

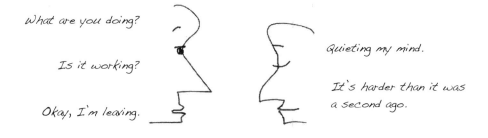

There are many names for the two voices that live in our heads. Here is a long list of them, many of which will be discussed in the pages that follow. Take some time with this list in order to understand which types of thinking are worldly and which are sacred.

World(ly) voice	Sacred voice
Mental Static Self-talk, Automatic Thinking, Internal Dialogue, Inner Roommate, Mind-talk, Incessant Monologue	**Silence** Quietness, "Still, Small Voice," Inner Voice, Inner Guidance, Wisdom, Inner Knowing, Inner Spirit, Seat of Consciousness, Center, Enlightened Soul, Unconditional Love
Reactive Mind Monkey Mind, Devil Talk, Trickster, Criticism, Complaining, The (Wo)Man Inside, Gossip, Think It Through **Head Games** Calculating, Sense-making, Reason-giving, Restlessness, Louder and Faster, Racing Thoughts **Thinking Traps** Boxed-in, Trapped Impossibility (I can't), Survival (I have to), Obligation (I ought to, am supposed to), Desire to prove (I have to please) Illusion, Delusion, Jumping to Conclusions, Self-righteousness Judging ("shoulds"), Expectations, Demands, Emotional Reasoning, All or Nothing Thinking	**Proactive Mind** Wise Mind, Higher Mind, Divinity, Intelligent Force, First Cause, The Unmoving Mover, The Eternal, The All, The Presence, Great Intelligence, Faith, Grace **Freedom** Seeing with the Heart, Inspiration, Creativity, Radical Acceptance, Willingness, Certain Truth, Playfulness, Zero Expectations, Surrender, Allowing
Duality Time, "The Measurer," Localized, Fragmented, Partialness (in Parts), Polarized, Separateness	**Timelessness** The Divinity of Infinity, Whole, Complete, Non-Local, Open, Unity, Synthesis, Equilibrium, Balance, Ever-new Joy, Eternal Hope, Integrated, Connected
Being on Automatic Taking Your Life for Granted	**Present** The Moment, Being, Completely Doing, Receptivity, Honesty, Humility, Gratitude
Core lies Selfish, Proud, Guilty, Ego, Fated to Despair, Attacks on Self	**Core truth** Able, Strong, Worthy, Enough, Knowing, Destiny
Leads to: anger, anxiety, fear, confusion, sadness. Also leads to: temporary excitement, happiness, relief	**Leads to:** serenity, peacefulness, bliss, salvation

HEARING THE WORLDLY VOICE

Practice noticing how your thoughts are not you.

To Live Yes, it is valuable to practice slowing our thinking and taking a close look. It works like this. First there is an event (situation) that gets the self-talk going. In Hamlet's famous "to be or not to be" speech, Shakespeare referred to "the thousand natural shocks that flesh is heir to." Most of us could probably reach a thousand such shocks in a week! They keep coming all day, from the sound of the alarm clock to feeling a last little pain before we fall asleep.

Let's pick one to show how the mind reacts. For instance, imagine the moment that you notice that you don't have enough money in your account to pay your power bill. The self-talk starts immediately: "I thought I had enough. I don't make enough money. I should not have bought those shoes. I'll have to sit in the dark. I'll never get out of debt. It's not my fault. The world is rigged against me. Since I can't pay my bills, I am a waste of human space. I'm not good enough. I am incapable, worthless." All of this self-talk is the way your mind says "No" to what is happening in your life. To free yourself from the worldly voice, first identify the self-talk, and second, see if the talk itself is true or not. Don't forget that most of the worldly voice is a bald-faced lie.

Here's an exercise: Remember the specific words used by someone that triggered anger, anxiety, or sadness in you, and write them. Use the exact words and the exact time they were said. Now, while thinking about these words and feeling these feelings, write every thought that comes into your head. Look for every time you didn't like what you heard. Perhaps you can also find some self-criticism in your thoughts. Write it all on the page. Now go back and see if you can identify which thoughts you might be able to challenge – either because you don't know they're one hundred percent true or because they are false. The idea of a "thought record" was introduced when Dr. Aaron T. Beck created CBT in the early 1960s, and we will be using a unique version of it to shift from No to Yes.

Thought records help you practice slowing your thoughts and recognizing your own feelings. You may focus on something that happened recently or something that happened in your past. Most important is to do these processes on a regular basis, so you can get good at them. Below are a blank and a completed example of a basic thought record:

~~~~~~

EXERCISE—THE THOUGHT RECORD PROCESS   ☒

~~~~~~

1. Write one situation (specific words, specific time/place).

2. Write and feel your emotions, such as Mad, Sad, Scared, Confused, Bored. Rate each emotion from 0 to 100.

3. List the thoughts that led to that feeling. Rapidly list all the thoughts (self-talk) that you can think of. Stay in the memory. This may take pages.

4. Come back to the present. Take a breath.

5. Go back to the thoughts list, and challenge each thought while staying in the present. Write whether each thought is True (T), False (F), Don't Know (DK).

6. Reflect on the thoughts and on how many were False.

~~~~~~

Exercise— The Thought Record Process

ONE SITUATION	EMOTIONS	THOUGHTS	P A U S E / T F DK	REFLECTIONS ON THE ACTUAL THOUGHTS
What was going on at the exact time you noticed your mood change? (Exact words, sensation, time, physical details)	What emotional feeling(s) did you experience? (Rate on a scale of 0-100) (Do this quickly.)	What thought(s) ran through your mind? What did that situation mean to you? What core lies came up about yourself? (Write a lot! Use more pages.)	P T A U F S E DK	How many of the thoughts are true? How many thoughts show that you are not accepting the original situation? How can you change those thoughts for the better?

Here is a completed example.

ONE SITUATION	EMOTIONS	THOUGHTS	P A U S E	REFLECTIONS ON THE ACTUAL THOUGHTS
What was going on at the exact time you noticed your mood change? (Exact words, sensation, time, physical details)	What emotional feeling(s) did you experience? Rate on a scale of 0-100 (Do this quickly.)	What thought(s) ran through your mind? What did that situation mean to you? What core lies came up about yourself? (Write a lot! Use more pages.)	T — F — DK	How many of the thoughts are true? How many thoughts show that you are not accepting the original situation? How can you change those thoughts for the better?
Yesterday after dinner, my wife said, "You're getting so fat, we have to widen the door."	Annoyed 100 Angry 90 Disgusted 100	She's riding me.	DK	This is my perception.
		She's insensitive.	F	Sometimes she understands me.
		I'm okay like I am.	T	I am okay like I am because there's no other way to be.
		I do not need to lose weight.	F	I would be healthier at a lower weight.
		She's always negative.	F	She is sometimes positive.
		She doesn't care about me.	F	She cares enough to not leave me.

Don't be concerned if this exercise is difficult at first. Few of us have been taught how to challenge our thoughts. It takes practice. As you continue to write Thought Record Processes and recognize that all or most of your self-talk is not true, you will begin to notice that your anger, anxiety, or sadness levels go down. As you continue to learn more ways to Live Yes, you will improve your ability to slow your thinking.

As with all these ideas, Living Yes is a choice that you may make at any time. It's not always obvious where the Yes is, but once you can find the No and get to the Yes, you can change yourself and find mental and emotional freedom in an instant.

Although clearing your thinking is helpful in making decisions, this exercise is not about solving the problem. It is an honest look at your false thinking. Clearing the mind in this way may help you problem-solve later, but if you skip over your muddy "No" thinking to find the solution before you say "Yes" to the problem, the process will fail and the solution to the problem may not work either.

THINKING TRAPS

Your mind can trick you.

As we develop our mind's ability to break free from traps, more traps appear. The lie is the trap. It seems like a never-ending attack from the outside and a closed-in cage from the inside.

We may get trapped when we believe a situation is impossible. We may get trapped when we fear for our survival. We may get trapped by doing what we think someone else said we should be doing, either recently or in our distant memory. We may get trapped when we make efforts to prove ourselves worthy to others. We shut down when we listen too much to our inner critic. All those beliefs keep us from experiencing our own freedom.

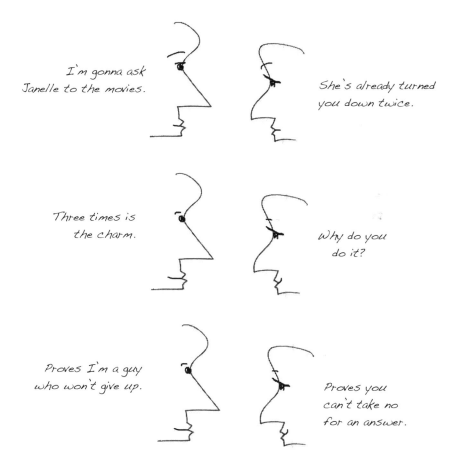

You Live Yes more easily when you keep yourself mentally flexible instead of getting trapped by your rigid thinking. Just like warming up before exercising, you stay in the best condition when you do not get stuck in rigid thinking traps. When your mind is loose, you're ready to respond, ready for action.

When you are under stress, your mind messes up more. You predict the future. You assume everything will turn out badly. You decide how things should be. You judge how things are. You take everything personally. Sometimes, when you are in the heat of an emotion, you believe the crazy thoughts that made you angry, sad, or afraid. You interpret events as all or nothing. You take a small event and assume it's a never-ending pattern. You conclude that a small detail represents a whole movement. You believe a label. Those thinking traps prevent you from Living Yes. The result is lots of unnecessary suffering.

So, if your thoughts are not always true, how do you decide which thoughts to believe? One way is to examine the four thinking traps. (I first learned the term "thinking traps" from Dr. Amy Wenzel, and I have combined them into four types.)

THE FOUR THINKING TRAPS
Break it down into four types.

1. Jumping to Conclusions (JTC)

You cannot predict the future with 100% accuracy. You cannot know what others are thinking. You are not a fortuneteller or a mind reader. Stop pretending otherwise.

2. Judgment (J)

"Should" statements or judgments are poor motivators and ugly punishers. You do not need to be so hard on yourself. Leave Big Judgments to your Higher Power, so you may give yourself and those around you a break. When you label other people or situations, you are judging them. For example, if the clerk at the DMV is "mean," you become trapped in Big Judgment and have lost your compassion. When you judge yourself, you lose compassion for yourself as well.

3. Emotional Reasoning (ER)

Your thoughts and feelings often get tangled together. If you are feeling angry, you are probably going to be quick to conclude that events are working against you. If you're feeling scared, you are likely to conclude that events are threatening your safety. It is usually better to calm down before you examine your thinking.

4. All or Nothing Thinking (Aor0)

The world is not all or nothing, black and white. Often you ignore the positive or decide that a series of events means total disaster when that is not necessarily true. If you over-generalize one scary detail and conclude that it means everything is dangerous, you'll always be anxious. If you don't have enough money to pay a bill, that does not mean you can never pay your bills again and that you're a useless person. It only means that you don't have the money right now.

THOUGHT RECORDS AND THE FOUR THINKING TRAPS

Presenting the master cognitive process.

Now we're going to go bigger. We are going to add the thinking traps to the thought record process. The complete process will appear in a few pages. Here's how to do it: Use a small distressing event. Be specific about the situation. What time was it? What words were spoken? Pick one or more of the five feelings: mad, sad, scared, confused, bored. Scale them from 0 to 100. Now write everything that is in your head. Include all the reactive mind chatter, hateful words, and accusations. You don't have to solve any problems, just get to the No here. Look at the four thinking traps and, next to each thought, write as many of the traps as you can. Use the abbreviations JTC, J, ER, Aor0.

There are only seven abbreviations used in this process: the four thinking traps – JTC, J, ER, Aor0; and the three possible outcomes for each thought – T, F, DK. If you learn them, you will be able to work the upcoming process more easily.

> JTC: jumping to conclusions
> J: judgment
> ER: emotional reasoning
> Aor0: all or nothing thinking
> T: true
> F: false
> DK: don't know

Identifying the thinking traps helps you see if your self-talk is true (T), false (F), or don't know (DK). Jumping to conclusions (JTC) is always DK (don't know) because the future is unknowable. Judgment (J), emotional reasoning (ER), and all or nothing thinking (Aor0) lead to false (F) thoughts.

Once you have identified the thinking traps and T/F/DK, Live Yes by writing the truthful alternative for each thought. Remember that the context of the situation is probably not the only way to look at it. Break free of that context! Use facts when possible and use the thought traps as clues to where your thinking was not useful.

Once you have found a truthful alternative for each thought, examine the outcome. Look at your emotions again, and see if their intensity has dropped. Perhaps a frustration level of 80 dropped to 30. If so, the exercise is working. Write the new emotional rating as the outcome, and, as you're seeing things more clearly, consider what you now choose to do. Perhaps you will choose an activity, or perhaps you will see yourself behaving in the future in a more healthful way.

For example, Bill might be upset that last night at 7 p.m. Janelle turned him down for a date. He finds himself annoyed at level 100, angry at level 60, and sad at level 45. He lists his thoughts that were triggered by the situation such as "She doesn't get me. She's not good enough for me. Nobody will ever go out with me. I'm not capable of getting a girlfriend. She's a bitch. I'm no good. She should go out with me." He fills several pages with reactive thoughts like those. Then he takes a breath and pauses. Now he goes through each of his thoughts, identifies one of the four the thinking traps (JTC, J, ER, Aor0) and uses the abbreviations T, F, or DK, then writes a truthful alternative for each thought. It might look like this:

"She doesn't get me." | JTC (jumping to conclusions) DK (don't know) | "I can't read her mind. I don't know if she gets me or not. I just know she said no."

"She's not good enough for me." | J (judgment) F (false) | "That's a defensive thought on my part. She's good enough for me to ask out. Not everyone will be willing to go out with me."

"Nobody will ever go out with me." | JTC (jumping to conclusions), ER (emotional reasoning) F (false) | "I can't know that, and it's pretty unlikely no one will ever want to go out with me again."

"I'm not capable of getting a girlfriend." | Aor0 (all or nothing thinking) F (false) | "I've had girlfriends in the past, and when it's the right time, I'll likely have one again."

"She's a bitch." | J (judgment), ER (emotional reasoning), Aor0 (all or nothing thinking) F (false) | "This is my anger talking. She's been perfectly nice in the way she said no. And even if she wasn't, that doesn't mean she's *always* a bitch. It's my defensiveness labeling her."

"I'm no good." | J (judgment), Aor0 (all or nothing thinking) F (false) | "I am a good person and I was strong enough to ask her out. Now my mind is attacking me instead of her, but it's still a lie. I am perfectly capable."

"She should go out with me." | J (judgment), F (false) | "I don't know this. I am not all-knowing and honestly have no idea what should happen. It's possible that this wouldn't work out, and she's saved me the grief."

Bill realizes that his annoyance is now down to zero, his anger has gone down to 10, and his sadness is down to 15. As he continues to reflect on the truth of the situation, he realizes that she may have many reasons to say no to him that have nothing to do with his thoughts. Perhaps she has a boyfriend, or she's not dating, or he was too aggressive with her. These alternative possibilities allow him to recognize how his thoughts may be thinking traps, and the result is that he feels more relaxed.

Now work on an expanded version of the process. Writing a thought record provides an opportunity to challenge your thoughts, take a stand on what is true, and decide your next move. There is also an example. If you can master completing these, you will have the skill to overcome the chatter in your head and become clear thinking. Remember, getting good at this takes a lot of practice!

EXERCISE—DEVELOPING ALTERNATIVE THOUGHTS ☒

Part One (relive a memory):

1. Write One Situation per form.

2. Write the Emotions with ratings.

3. Write all the Thoughts that led to the feeling. Write rapidly, but keep going and going.

* Pause

4. Come back to the present. Take a breath.

Part Two (in present):

5. Review each Thought and assign a Thinking Trap, T/F/DK, and a Truthful Alternative for Each Thought. Then do the next pair (Thinking Traps, T/F/DK, Truthful Alternative for Each Thought).

6. Review the Outcome. For each emotion assign a new rating number. Once clear, write what action you now choose to take or visualize.

ONE SITUATION	EMOTIONS	THOUGHTS	P A U S E	THINKING TRAPS	T I F I DK	TRUTHFUL ALTERNATIVE FOR EACH THOUGHT	OUTCOME
What was going on at the exact time you noticed your mood change? (Exact words, sensation, time, physical details)	What emotional feeling(s) did you experience? (Rate on a scale of 0-100) (Do this quickly.)	What thought(s) ran through your mind? What did that situation mean to you? What core lies came up about yourself? (Write a lot! Use more pages.)		Examples: Jumping to Conclusions (=DK), Judgment (=F), Emotional Reasoning (=F), All or Nothing Thinking (=F) (Go straight across to Truth telling for each.)		Aware of the thinking traps, answer each thought with evidence-based, rational responses using facts, data, or actual events. How can you restate this thought so you may choose acceptance, humility, honesty, self-love, or openness? Write the truth.	Re-rate your emotions from the Emotions Column (with the rating scale) and write what course of action you will take. Visualize yourself behaving clearly and telling the truth in a similar situation
	NO	MOSTLY NO				LIVING YES	LIVING YES

Notice how when we are in memory and wrapped in our thoughts and feelings, we are saying "No." Once we challenge our thinking with thinking traps and declare the truth, we can choose to Live Yes with alternative thoughts and clear outcomes.

Please review the example of a full-blown thought record on the next page.

ONE SITUATION	EMOTIONS	THOUGHTS	P A U S E	THINKING TRAPS	T I F I D K	TRUTHFUL ALTERNATIVE FOR EACH THOUGHT	OUTCOME
What was going on at the exact time you noticed your mood change? (Exact words, sensation, time, physical details)	What emotional feeling(s) did you experience? (Rate on a scale of 0-100) (Do this quickly.)	What thought(s) ran through your mind? What did that situation mean to you? What core lies came up about yourself? (Write a lot! Use more pages.)		Examples: Jumping to Conclusions (=DK), Judgment (=F), Emotional Reasoning (=F), All or Nothing Thinking (=F) (Go straight across to Truth telling for each.)		Aware of the thinking traps, answer each thought with evidence-based, rational responses using facts, data, or actual events. How can you restate this thought so you may choose acceptance, humility, honesty, self-love, or openness? Write the truth.	Re-rate your emotions from the Emotions Column (with the rating scale) and write what course of action you will take. Visualize yourself behaving clearly and telling the truth in a similar situation
Yesterday after dinner, my wife said, "You're getting so fat, we have to widen the door."	Annoyed 100 Angry 90 Disgusted 100	She's riding me. She's insensitive. I'm okay like I am. I do not need to lose weight. She's always negative. She doesn't care about me		ER J, A/0 ER, J A/0 JTC, J	D K F T F F F	She just said a few words, and I got mad at her. Just because she said I'm overweight, doesn't mean she's insensitive. I'm okay like I am. I could consider it. Sometimes she's positive, especially when I bring home a paycheck. She cooks and stays with me.	Annoyed 30 Angry 20 Disgusted 5 I am not going to let her ruin my day. If I get upset again, I am going to go to a quiet place and do another process. I am going to go to the doctor and see if he recommends a weight loss program.

Thinking traps come from self-righteousness or self-rightness. What's true for me may not be true for you. If you are proving your rightness, you leave no room for compassion, sound judgment, or openness to what is offered by the universe.

How you think leads to how you live. As Life challenges you to Live Yes, you can notice patterns of obstacles that arise. By Living Yes, you can take responsibility for what's going on in your head and what you perceive outside of your head.

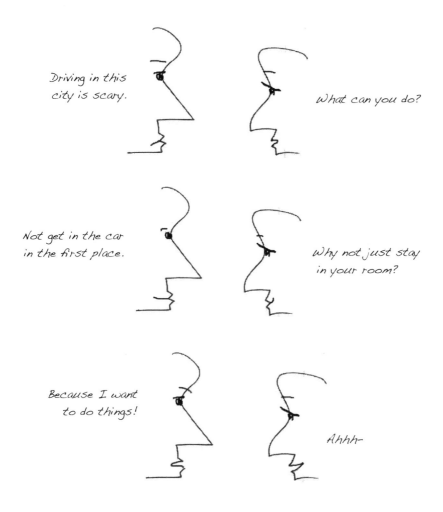

PROGRESS CHECK

Can you hear the worldly voices in your head right now? What are they saying?

Have you ever heard the sacred voice? If so, how did you feel at the time?

Write five full thought record processes (developing alternative thoughts) in one week. What did you notice?

Can you point out thinking traps when your automatic thoughts come up?

Write five thought record processes per week for a month.

What have you learned about your automatic thoughts?

Are there parts of the book that you skipped, including the progress check questions, because you are not ready to change? Are you ready now?

5 Feelings and Thoughts

WHAT IS A FEELING?

Understanding human architecture begins with learning the difference between thinking and feeling.

Are you the type of person who lives more in your head or your heart? Are you more of a thinker or a feeler? Thinking and feeling are closely related, but they are not the same. Being able to know the difference is important.

The looser meanings of the word "feeling" that have come into use in the last 50 years are often at the center of the confusion. In English, "feeling" once meant either a physical sensation, like the feelings in my hands, or an emotional experience, like feeling anxious about someone else. Nowadays, "feel" and "feeling" have expanded to include thoughts, beliefs, opinions, hunches, and intuitions. Feeling that your life is too short is a belief, which is a thought. Having a feeling that someone is dangerous relies on our intuition, which invites thought and emotion.

Since thoughts and feelings are both wrapped in the word "feel," we will use the word "feeling" to describe only emotions (like "glad, mad, sad, scared, confused, bored") and physical states. We will not use the word feel to describe our thoughts or beliefs. "I feel you meant to hurt me" is a thought that we would say as "I think you meant to hurt me," or "I believe you meant to hurt me."

Here is a chart that shows the important difference between thinking and feeling.

Chart — Thoughts versus Feelings

Thinking=belief=cognition	Feeling=emotion=instinct=mood
Thinking states	Arousal states
Front brain, cerebral, or "intelligence"	Midbrain, limbic brain, instinct
Monkey brain	Lizard brain
Fast to thinking brain	Even faster to instinct brain
May not be true	Always true

For example, being mad is an emotion. The emotion exists in real time, in the here-and-now, and is absolute. When we're mad, we're mad.

Why we're mad is subject to our own interpretation, so "why" is a thought, and the thought may not be true. Figuring out why you're mad is a thought. The statement "I'm mad because I'm late" shows an emotion that comes from a thought. The meaning you put on being late (thought) caused you to become mad (emotion).

THOUGHTS VERSUS FEELINGS QUIZ   ☒

Telling the difference between a thought and a feeling may be harder than it looks. These ten words are either thoughts or feelings. Circle the correct answer.

1. Abandoned   Thought or Feeling?

2. Afraid   Thought or Feeling?

3. Aggressive   Thought or Feeling?

4. Aggravated   Thought or Feeling?

5. Alienated   Thought or Feeling?

6. Angry   Thought or Feeling?

7. Accurate   Thought or Feeling?

8. Annoyed   Thought or Feeling?

9. Approving   Thought or Feeling?

10. Anxious   Thought or Feeling?

(Answer – the odd numbered items are thoughts and the even numbered items are feelings.)

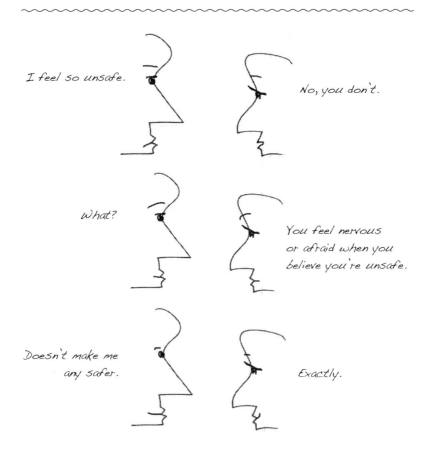

Emotion is arousal. Science points to the so-called "four f's" of arousal: feeding (consuming), fleeing (fear), fighting (anger), and mating (sex). Emotional intensity comes from the depth of your belief. "How deeply do you feel that?" means "how much do you believe that?" Being more ready to fight does not necessarily mean you are more passionate. It may be you are not thinking very clearly.

Your thoughts are fast and many. Most of them happen instantly and outside of your awareness. Because you don't have time to filter your thoughts before they happen, they become confused with feelings. As you learned in the last chapter, because your thoughts are not necessarily true, you can challenge them and create a helpful result by claiming alternative thoughts.

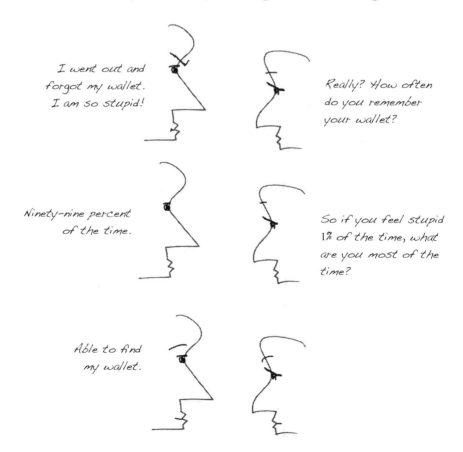

USING THE DIFFERENCE BETWEEN THOUGHTS AND FEELINGS

Thoughts often lie. Feelings never lie.

Thinking and feeling states are different from each other. Thoughts put us in verbal self-defense with endless battles inside ourselves. Feelings are simply true.

The *truth test* is useful in determining whether an idea is a thought or a feeling. If it can be challenged, it's a thought. As we learned in the last chapter, thinking traps cause False and Don't Know thinking. Yet, emotional states are absolutely true. Knowing this difference can help us identify our feelings. It is a valuable skill to be able to use feeling words to describe what is true.

Our language has developed around thoughts and has many words for them. Yet, there are few words used to describe emotion, and even these few words don't describe emotion very well. To some people, for example, "anger" means an uncomfortable emotion just short of rage. However, the word "anger" is also used to describe a full range of the feeling from annoyed to irritated to mad to angry to raging.

The jingle "mad, sad, glad, scared, confused, bored" will identify most of the feelings. (If we add "shock, disgust, calm, excited, ashamed, and curious," we have boiled down feeling states into twelve words.)

The chart on the following page lists six feelings with intensity words from low to high.

Knowing how we feel is an important part of every moment. Many of us have difficulty identifying how we feel. We cut ourselves off from who we are when we buy in to the pull-it-up-by-the-bootstraps, John Wayne, tough and independent, not-bogging-down-in-wimpy-tears position of our male-dominated society. But emotions are real. Awareness of them invites us to

Chart — Intensity of Feelings

MAD: bored, irritated, annoyed, frustrated, angry, furious, enraged
SAD: low, mild grief, hurt, despair, agony
GLAD: amused, glad, happy, joyous, ecstatic
SCARED: worried, nervous, anxious, afraid, terrified, panicked
EXCITED: curious, aroused, orgasmic
ASHAMED: reserved, shy, embarrassed, humiliated

Live Yes with our whole selves. The alternative is avoidance, which results in a constant state of No. Not acknowledging a feeling is a way to say "No." Denying an emotion is a way to say "No." Admitting how we feel emotionally is a clear way to Live Yes.

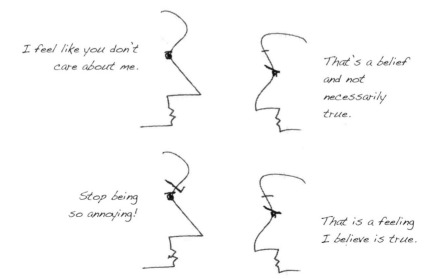

I feel like you don't care about me.

That's a belief and not necessarily true.

Stop being so annoying!

That is a feeling I believe is true.

Sometimes we use vague words to avoid feelings altogether, such as: "good, bad, great, okay, fine, so-so." Such words are so weak that they don't describe anything real, so they let us avoid. Using those avoiding words is a way to say "No." To sum up: the statement "I feel good about myself" is vague and not even about feelings.

Here is an exercise that will help you learn to ground yourself in truth and improve your ability to express yourself clearly.

EXERCISE – PRACTICE IDENTIFYING FEELINGS   ⊠

Many times each day, scan your body and identify how you feel. Find a word that describes your current emotional state, and write it. Do not include reasons for the feeling or beliefs about what the feeling means, just write the emotion. Use the jingle, the full twelve words or the Intensity of Feelings chart on p.79 as a tool to accomplish this practice until you don't need it any more. You may also scale the intensity of the feeling from 0 to 100.

It might look like this: When you wake up you may feel "confused 50." At breakfast you may feel "excited 25" and "anxious 45." At mid-morning you may feel "irritated 30" and "anxious 45." At lunch you may feel "relief 25." At mid-afternoon you may feel "ashamed 90" and "angry 100." During late afternoon you may feel "sad 30." On your way home from work you may feel "annoyed 80" and "anxious 45," and when you arrive home, you may feel "annoyed 55" and "excited 30." Before sleep you may feel "relief 75" and "anxious 25." And as you drift off to bed you may feel "joy 20."

THOUGHTS PRODUCE FEELINGS

Use the principle of cognitive theory.

A popular system of therapy developed by Dr. Beck, Dr. Ellis, and others is called "cognitive theory" (CT). CT examines the relationship between our thoughts and our feelings. In Living Yes terms, CT looks like this:

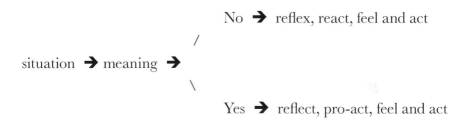

When an event or situation occurs, we have only an instant to interpret the meaning of the situation before our thinking sweeps us into a reaction. That choice, to Live Yes or not, determines how we experience the event or situation.

Knowing that your thoughts produce your feelings is a huge advantage. You may use your feelings to find out what you think, or you may look at your thoughts to figure out what you feel. With practice, you will be able to challenge your self-talk, slow your mind, and not react as emotionally.

For example, while in traffic you may either blame the drivers and the traffic and become irritated, or you may change the meaning. You might see the traffic as an opportunity to relax, to go with the flow. You might use the time to listen to lovely music and stay relaxed. The way you view the situation results in how you feel. In this case, the way you think about the traffic (Yes or No) results in the feeling of being either irritated or relaxed.

The exercise also can work in reverse. If you identify your feeling of irritation, you may look at the thought that brought you there. Demanding that automobile drivers be more respectful, or fewer, or faster, or slower, or whatever is underneath your anger will give you a guide to where you may change your thoughts to improve your mood. Living Yes with the traffic will result in finding the thought and then feeling relief. Holding the No will result in continued or increased irritation. If you expect something to happen (a thought), and it doesn't (reality), you will become frustrated (a feeling) or disappointed (a feeling).

In Chapter Four we introduced thought records. The lists of destructive thoughts you made helped you see a way to think more clearly and then change your painful emotional responses. By making a clear choice, you may reduce your painful emotions and open yourself to the connecting and sacred. Remember, it looks like this:

ONE SITUATION	EMOTIONS	THOUGHTS	P A U S E	THINKING TRAPS	T I F I DK	TRUTHFUL ALTERNATIVE FOR EACH THOUGHT	OUTCOME
What was going on at the exact time you noticed your mood change? (Exact words, sensation, time, physical details)	What emotional feeling(s) did you experience? (Rate on a scale of 0-100) (Do this quickly.)	What thought(s) ran through your mind? What did that situation mean to you? What core lies came up about yourself? (Write a lot! Use more pages.)		Examples: Jumping to Conclusions (=DK), Judgment (=F), Emotional Reasoning (=F), All or Nothing Thinking (=F) (Go straight across to Truth telling for each.)		Aware of the thinking traps, answer each thought with evidence-based, rational responses using facts, data, or actual events. How can you restate this thought so you may choose acceptance, humility, honesty, self-love, or openness? Write the truth.	Re-rate your emotions from the Emotions Column (with the rating scale) and write what course of action you will take. Visualize yourself behaving clearly and telling the truth in a similar situation

It is important to practice these thought record processes often, even if you think you understand Living Yes completely. By writing your thoughts and the alternatives, you may get access to what Dr. Beck calls "reflective thoughts." (He calls automatic thoughts "reflexive thoughts.") The thought record processes are the most significant tools used in cognitive theory. They help you convert your thinking from (automatic) reflex to (considered) reflection.

SEPARATED OR CONNECTED.

Feelings can be connecting or separating and can teach us what we care about.

Emotions teach us about our thoughts and are useful, even when they hurt. Feelings such as joy, gratitude, happiness, or calm connect us to the world. Feelings, such as anger, shame, sadness and fear lock us into the false idea that we are broken off from the rest of the world.

Connecting emotions such as love or gratitude offer us an opportunity to deepen our humanity. Separating emotions such as anger or anxiety also offer us an opportunity to deepen our humanity. Any time we experience a separating emotion, we are saying "No" and have an opportunity to learn how to Live Yes.

Learning to accept your sadness or grief is better than falsely replacing these feelings with emotions such as joy or relief. You don't always have to connect. Sometimes you want to separate. Being angry, sad, or afraid is disconnecting, but it's real. It's alright to feel whatever you feel, even when it's uncomfortable and disconnecting.

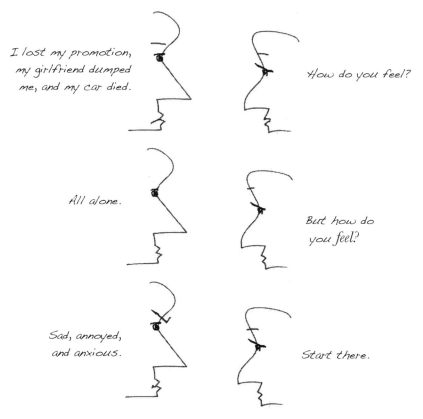

Some people believe in good and bad or in positive and negative emotions, but all feelings are a gift of being human. Separating emotions come from false thoughts, but that does not make them wrong or useless. Separating emotions often mean you have blocked access to your own spirituality. Fighting against a separating emotion is a way to say "No." With anger, for example, stuffing the feeling instead of finding a safe way to release it causes additional pain. When you honestly experience your pain, you are saying "Yes," but if you avoid or hurt others with your pain, it causes more pain. Not being willing to forgive can be a block which keeps you angry for a long time.

Shame breaks you down when you want too much from other people and not enough from your higher self. Grief and sadness show you what you care about. They offer you a chance to open your heart to grow into a lovely lover who may connect with any living soul. Boredom or feeling a void inside can mean that you are not in touch with the living universe, sometimes called "God" or a "Higher Power."

Being frustrated or annoyed suggests that you want to change a past event which cannot be changed. Anger is useful because it shows you what you are having trouble tolerating and where you need to set boundaries. Acceptance is the best way to relieve yourself from anger. Living Yes cannot happen without total acceptance. Reality happens, and anger is the result of what you don't like, but the event happened and the anger came out. No matter how hard you may try, you cannot change the past.

Anxiety, worry, and fear are failed attempts to control the future. Control will not work because you are only human. Outside events will happen that are potentially dangerous. Fear has a benefit because it helps you to get away from danger and to protect yourself. But when you have done all you can, fear no longer serves you. Because fears come from your No reactions, you can work to overcome fear by striving to truly Live Yes. We will discuss more about how to learn from separating emotions in the next chapter.

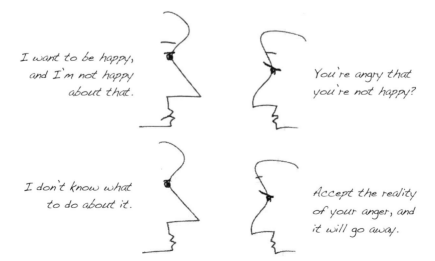

I want to be happy, and I'm not happy about that.

You're angry that you're not happy?

I don't know what to do about it.

Accept the reality of your anger, and it will go away.

Chart – The Moment Model

The only way to Live Yes is in the moment. Constantly chose to live your life right here, right now. If you are able to keep your mind on the wonders of the present moment, you will be able to listen to your sacred inner voice. Unfortunately, it is easy to stray into the past or future.

There is a relationship between being right here, right now and how you feel. Thinking about the past without accepting the realities of the present leads to separating emotions such as anger, shame, and sadness. Thinking about the future with thoughts such as demanding control can provoke anxiety and fear. And sometimes when you cannot tolerate the present, your thoughts block you and leave you confused, emotionally flooded, or bored. Here is the model.

PRESENT THOUGHT (YES)
Being
Right here right now
In the Zone
The Now
Happy, Joyous, and Free
Mindful
Aware
Spirit
Doing

PAST THOUGHT	(NO)	FUTURE THOUGHT
Anger		**Anxiety/Fear**
tied to unmet expectations		unsafe belief about the future
judgments triggering lies		belief past dangers will repeat
Shame		
judgments triggering lies		
Sadness		

BLOCKED FROM PRESENT THOUGHT

ruminating about losses	**Confused** **Bored**
judgments triggering lies	**Emotionally flooded**
	disconnected from the present

As you have probably figured out by now, feelings, thoughts, and actions are useful in learning how to change saying "No" into saying "Yes." Because we can trace our thoughts backwards from our feelings, we can use this knowledge to Live Yes.

After we work on enough thought records and practice living in the present moment, we notice our thinking begins to change while a situation is happening. We notice when we are saying "Yes" to what just happened. We feel whatever comes and experience "Yes," even when it feels separating. We catch many of our "No" thoughts right then and immediately realize how we can tell the truth about each of them. This means that we can take a stand on how to act with that deeper knowledge of what is happening. By living truth in the context of the moment, we are practicing Living Yes in real time.

In the following exercise, you use feelings, thoughts, and behaviors as your guideposts to trace back to the original idea that got you into a Stuck-in-No pattern. By identifying where you are holding yourself back, you may begin the voyage of Living Yes.

EXERCISE—THREE PLACES NOES LEAD AND TRACING IT BACK TO GET TO YES ⊠

1. NOES lead to separating feelings:

Anger, anxiety, sadness, frustration, annoyance, irritation, shock, fear, grief, confusion, disgust, shame, jealousy, rage, boredom, loneliness.

Trace it back. Ask: When did it begin?

2. NOES lead to trapped thinking:

Don't like something.

Don't want something.

Blaming other people; it's their fault.

Blaming systems (machines, corporations, government, the universe, God).

Trace it back. Ask: When did it begin?

The situation seems impossible to get out of.

The situation seems to require action to ensure your very survival.

The situation seems to obligate you to act in a way you don't like.

The situation calls for you to want to prove to others that you are okay.

Trace it back. Ask: When did it begin?

3. NOES lead us to behaviors:

Slumping, tightening up, getting tired, not moving, indulging.

Complaining, criticizing, gossiping, pouting.

Talking faster or slower than usual.

Talking louder or softer than usual.

Talking a lot more than usual.

Talking a lot less than usual.

Giving answers for everything.

Acting in ways you don't like (driving too fast, slamming doors, behaving rudely).

Withdrawing from others.

Trace it back. Ask: When did it begin?

Noticing others are behaving differently toward you.

Trace it back. Ask: When did it begin?

DRILLING DOWN

Underneath the mind chatter are hidden lies.

The voice in your head is long string of thoughts. Underneath the obvious thoughts are many hidden (unconscious) thoughts. The hidden beliefs and meanings create the stream of mental chatter. Those are the inflexible, false assumptions you have made about Life. They are rooted in the core lies you taught yourself since you were two or three years old. The core lies are the hidden mother lode upon which you have built a basis of fear of the world and of yourself. You rely on this false belief system to say No to Life. Here's how the hidden thoughts rise up.

Hidden Thoughts Model

Triggering Event	**Automatic Thoughts** Conscious mind chatter	**Response** Emotional Physical

Unconscious false **assumptions**
Inflexible **rules** and beliefs

Core Lies
False flaws

Hidden Thoughts Example

Triggering Event:	**Automatic Thoughts:**	**Response:**
Clock shows that report is due in one hour	"I have to get this right." "I can't show I'm not ready." "I'll make it so good that no one can judge me."	Anxiety: 90

Assumption: "I have to be perfect to prove I'm good enough."

Core Lie: "I'm inadequate."

To discover what is hidden, ask yourself what each of your thoughts means. Work your way down the Hidden Thoughts Model to identify the restrictions you put on yourself, the false beliefs and unnecessary rules you follow, and the core lies that rule you. This is called the "downward arrow technique." Here are some phrases you can use to drill down to discover the false assumptions and core lies.

… this thought means that the type of person I am is …

… this thought reveals that I am fundamentally flawed because I am …

… this thought exposes what's wrong with me, which is …

… this thought shows that I am accusing myself of being …

… if this thought is true, the worst that can happen is … which would mean that I am …

As you continue to write thought records and use the downward arrow technique, your hidden thoughts will gradually become more visible. This practice will shine light on the places you are Saying No and resisting Living Yes.

DOWN TO THE CORE

One day you taught yourself a lie that colored your world. Now it has turned you against yourself.

A "core lie" is the root of No. A core lie is the lie you told yourself as a child in order to cope with an unbearable situation. It is the lie to beat all lies. A core lie is the most self-destructive belief that you could find to make sense out of your pain. Everyone has them.

For example, if you had a demanding parent who always pushed you to be "perfect" (an expectation), you may have come to believe you weren't good enough, because that's what the repeated demands meant to you. Punishment of self and others often leads to anger and insecurity. Every time your mother said you had to wash because you were dirty, you may have heard, "I'm not clean enough, and I'm not good enough." She was the giant you depended on, so whatever she said had to be true. You took in a core lie as a way to make sense of being less than you thought she wanted.

Maybe you had a very easy-to-satisfy parent who did not push you enough. In your child mind, you decided this meant you didn't matter. From that you built a core lie that you were unlovable, worthless, or inadequate.

Victor Frankl said people "think too much" or "try too hard." That's it. Learn to think less by talking back to core lies. And learn to be a human being instead of a human doing. We will discuss being and mindfulness in the next chapter. Right now, let's examine how to talk back to core lies.

~~~~~~

EXERCISE— THE EIGHT CORE LIES (WAYS TO SAY "NO") WITH
TRUTH RESPONSE AFFIRMATIONS (LIVING YES)   ☒

~~~~~~

Read each core lie and response, and then fill in the blanks with evidence-based facts, data, or actual events.

Core lie #1: **I am unlovable.**

Living Yes response: Everyone is lovable. I am capable of attracting all the love I need.

Living Yes exercise: I am lovable because _____.

Core lie # 2: **I am weak.**

Living Yes response: Everyone has strengths. I can tap into the infinite strength of the universe.

Living Yes exercise: My strengths include _____.

Core lie # 3: **I am stupid.**

Living Yes response: I function my own way. I am wise enough. I know how to think clearly.

Living Yes exercise: I am smart in the following ways _____.

Core lie # 4: **I am worthless.**

Living Yes response: Everyone has worth. I am fully worthy as a mother / father / daughter / son / person.

Living Yes exercise: I am worthy because _____.

Core lie # 5: **I am broken.**

Living Yes response: I use what I have to live wholly, and do all that I am able.

Living Yes exercise: I am whole because _____.

Core lie # 6: **I am inadequate.**

Living Yes response: I am fine as I am. "God don't make junk."

Living Yes exercise: I am adequate because _____.

Core lie # 7: **I am unimportant.**

Living Yes response: I do my part as best I can. "I am God's good creation."

Living Yes exercise: I am important because _____.

Core lie # 8: **I am insignificant.**

Living Yes response: I am an essential part of the world. I do my part fully.

Living Yes exercise: I am significant because _____.

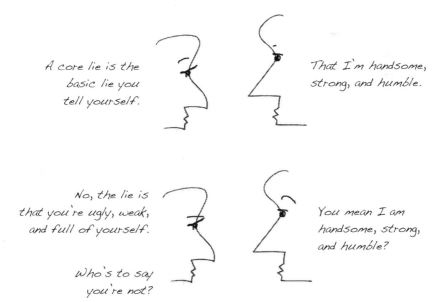

A core lie is the basic lie you tell yourself.

That I'm handsome, strong, and humble.

No, the lie is that you're ugly, weak, and full of yourself.

Who's to say you're not?

You mean I am handsome, strong, and humble?

PROGRESS CHECK

Can you name three feelings that are not thoughts?

Give an example in your life of how thoughts lie, but feelings do not.

Can you identify a thought that led to a feeling?

What feeling might you have had if you had a different thought about the situation?

Can you find the mental peace, if only for ten seconds, where you don't have any thoughts?

What happens to your feeling state when you do this?

Give an example where you have improved your ability to identify the No thoughts.

What are the rules and assumptions that you struggle with?

What are the most common core lies that you tell yourself when you are under stress?

What are the opposite core truths?

6 Feeling Emotions

ANGER HURTS

Anger is a painful way to prove you're right.

Anger is a general term for a separating emotion (the result of a No) that ranges from irritation to annoyance to frustration to anger to rage. The first step to learn about anger is how to manage your behavior by stopping the destructive urges to act out. Self-control and safe release are the best ways to deal with anger once it has begun. The second step to learn about anger is how to prevent it from starting in the first place.

ANGER MANAGEMENT (THE FIRST STEP)

Let go of anger.

Living Yes means we identify our anger and manage it in ways that do not hurt us or anyone else.

Once our anger is aroused, we are reacting. Our body becomes consumed with anger – elevated heart rate, sweat, red face, and racing thoughts. The angry emotion comes from our original brain wiring of "fight, flight, or freeze." Brain science says that when we become aroused in this way, we become absorbed, act on instinct, and think less clearly.

It is helpful to learn to become aware of our anger – both by noticing it while it's happening and by looking back at it afterwards. Practice using intensity scales, as you did in the last chapter, to help yourself notice your angry emotion. Say to yourself: "I was at an 80 out of 100 in my anger. Now I'm down to a 35." Choosing to become a master of your anger is an excellent way to Live Yes.

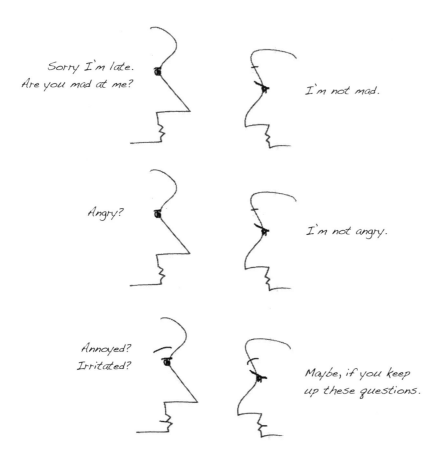

Sometimes Freud's old saying "Depression is anger turned inward" is true. Unexpressed anger can become sadness. Some use anger as a way to manipulate others. Some use anger to manipulate themselves! Sometimes the calmest-looking person in a room is the angriest. As we discussed in Chapter Five, some people deposit their anger onto others with passive-aggression. Successful management of anger does not mean not expressing anger. No matter what the type of anger, the practice of releasing anger in a healthful and constructive way is essential to a practice of Living Yes.

EXERCISE—RELEASING ANGER   ⊠

There are many skills we may use to safely release anger from the body. Techniques like these help us clear the air so we may return to a more relaxed mood and get a clear head.

- Take a time out (step away).

- Distract yourself by counting from 100 to 0 backwards by sevens.

- Gently pinch yourself on the hand between the thumb and first finger.

- Give yourself a finger massage or a jaw massage.

- Tune in to your breathing (slow, in-out belly breathing).

- Take three conscious breaths.

- Yell while alone such as inside a car with the music blaring.

- Punch a pillow.

- Do physical exercise such as shadow boxing, briskly walking, or lifting weights.

- Dance vigorously to loud music.

- Go to a place where you can yell and scream without worrying about being heard by others – in your car, in the woods, near a landing aircraft. Assert loudly, and shake your body and fists (but don't hurt yourself) while saying over and over again "I *won't* take it!" for 60 seconds. Pause for 30 seconds. Then assert loudly and shake while saying "I *will* take it!" over and over again for 60 seconds.

- This exercise is also a way to emotionally confront your core beliefs. Shaking your body/fists and say, "It's not true that I am (core lie)" for 60 seconds, then pause for 30 seconds, and then assert loudly and shake while saying, "It's true that I am (truth)" for 60 seconds. Do this daily for a magical 22 days until you fully believe it. Use the exact same phrases.

(More is written about releasing emotions in Chapter Nine.)

ANGER PREVENTION (THE SECOND STEP)

Live Yes before you choose anger.

As you learned in Chapter Five, the idea that the outside world makes us angry is not correct. Because you are the one who is putting meaning on the actions of others, you are responsible for your response. When your expectations are not met, you react with annoyance, frustration, fury, or rage.

Anger is a choice between accepting reality or saying "No" and indulging your destructive passion. Anger demands that your expectations be met. Anger reacts to your failure to control situations or people. When someone is in pain, Living Yes calls you to respond with something beyond your own anger or self-righteousness. No one can make you feel anger or self-righteousness. Instead, Live Yes by finding compassion. Seek (spiritual) truth rather than sensory indulgence, have zero expectations, and give up forcing what is out of your control and in the hands of your Higher Power. Choose to remain whole. Choose to not be ruffled. The choice is always yours.

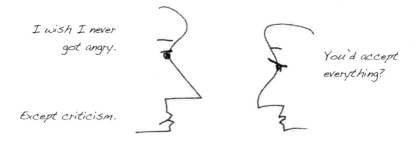

How do you choose to not be angry? Use thought records to examine the cause of your anger. If interpreting your mother-in-law's remark about some dirt on the floor creates a thought that you are unable to take care of her little boy, you might feel anger.

If her remark about the dirt triggers core lies such as that you are an unlovable person, you might feel anger. If her remark triggers a thought that you are an inadequate wife, you might feel anger. If you have a thought that you are a failure as a mother, you might feel anger. If you have a thought that you are an incapable homemaker, you might feel anger.

If, instead, you take the insults and examine your thoughts closely, you can stop the thoughts that provoke the anger. With practice you can reduce the anger itself. You can learn to make healthier thinking choices such as "I am a good wife," "I am doing the best I can," or "I am a child of the universe and doing pretty well claiming my joy." Thoughts such as these will stop you from creating more anger toward your mother-in-law. If you can see her behavior clearly, you may be able to see that her complaints reflect her own fears or her own self-destructive beliefs. This gives you a chance to not react to her complaints but instead to respond with compassion for her. You may choose to examine your own thinking. By Living Yes in this way, you have moved yourself from anger to compassion, and your mood improves.

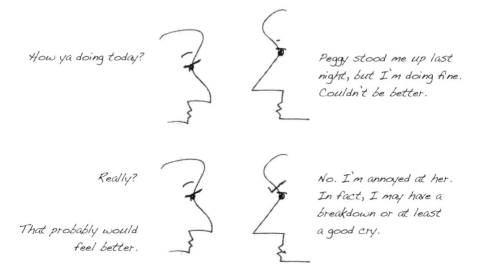

How ya doing today?

Peggy stood me up last night, but I'm doing fine. Couldn't be better.

Really?

That probably would feel better.

No. I'm annoyed at her. In fact, I may have a breakdown or at least a good cry.

Some people resist the idea that anger is a choice. They may be victims of the anger habit. As with any difficult habit, the anger pattern is often deep and requires time and effort to reverse. Substituting a positive behavior is the most effective way to break a habit. (More is written about positive choices in Chapter Seven.)

Anger has a purpose. It helps you understand what actions you don't like. Anger points to those parts of your life that you don't accept yet. It offers a valuable lesson. Anger shows you where your views do not meet reality. It is pointing to where you may evolve and grow into a complete, tolerant, and accepting person. It is showing you how to get to the No, so you may Live Yes. Anger has value; so do anxiety and stress.

ALONE AND AFRAID, ANXIETY AND STRESS

The more you struggle to control your future, the more pain you will feel.

Fear is a natural protector. By instinct, fear tells you to run from danger. Some amount of fear can be useful, but adding extra fear is unnecessary. Fear comes from thought about an event. Anxiety and stress come from constant fear. Sometimes you get stuck in a mental anxiety loop. The more anxious you get, the more tense your body gets, and the more tense your body gets, the more anxiety you feel.

I can't compete. It's dog-eat-dog out there.

What are you doing about it?

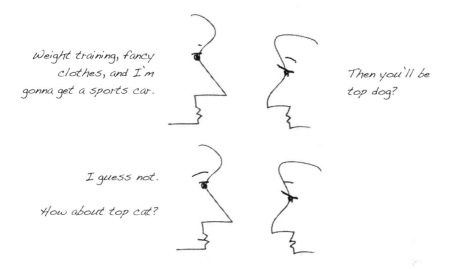

When you are afraid, you sometimes want to force results. You sometimes push to control your environment in order to get away from the fear. You sometimes push to control your run-away thoughts. The result is anxiety, stress, and symptoms such as panic attacks. A panic attack occurs when you react to your own physical response (such as a speedy heart beat, gasping for breath, sweating). If you believe that the reactions mean the situation is dangerous, a loop can form as you push to block out the world and control circumstances that cannot be controlled. Instead of naturally surrendering to the truth of the pain, you push to avoid feeling by tightening your control. The result is that you feel even more pain than when you started.

You keep worrying even though you know that worrying makes things worse. Sometimes you become stuck in your thoughts so deeply that you cannot see past your own fears. You become frozen in worries about the future. Fear is sometimes called false evidence appearing real. Just like a rabbit reacting to a wolf, your heart races, your blood pressure rises, your breath quickens, and you have to instantly decide whether to run ("flight"), fight or freeze. If you become overloaded with your fears and can't think straight, you are stuck in a No.

In this work, it is easy to look for things that make you scared. It is more challenging to let go of those fears, and find stress-free living. As actor Michael J. Fox was quoted saying, "There's no point in worrying because if something bad happens, then you've lived it twice."

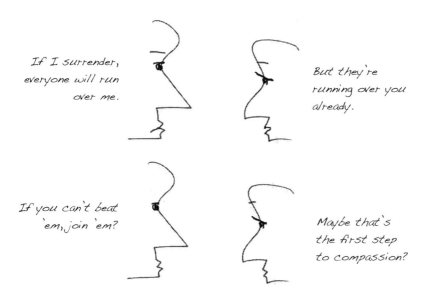

LIVING WITH COMPASSION

Live Yes with an open and vulnerable heart.

Selfish thinking leads us to suffering. Compassionate thinking leads us to peace. Outgrowing your fear and embracing compassion is a game changer. Do this by figuring out why the other person thinks he needs to be so scary. The more frightening he seems, the more afraid he is. Is he making himself big and scary to protect himself?

Realize that the more he tries to be scary, the more he is

crying out for compassion. We can see him as he is — a little, frightened child who is looking for someone who cares. Sadly he doesn't know how to surrender in order to feel. The more aggressive, loud, obnoxious, and scary he becomes, the more desperate he is for compassion. We can choose to Live Yes by seeing him this way and choose to Live Yes by offering compassion, not necessarily by saying anything, but by picturing his need. Being human means learning how to expand our love and compassion.

How well do you practice compassion? How often do you hold back your love or fail to forgive? When you are disappointed or annoyed with someone else's behavior, do you look for the good in others? Do you take responsibility for your own reaction to their behavior?

Recall that their fear and ignorance are driving them to behave in ways that feel separating. Recognize that when you feel annoyed or disappointed, you are not being open-hearted. As my friend Deb says, "If you get to know a person, any person, well enough, you will love them."

This is true for others, and it's true for you. If you knew your true self, you would love and be more compassionate toward yourself.

As with anger, there are two effective ways to deal with anxiety. The first is to immediately release stress through relaxation techniques such as those in the releasing anger exercise given earlier in this chapter. The other way is to not get wrapped in your thoughts or behaviors in the first place. Use thought records and other Living Yes exercises. Give up control and stop working to manipulate everything. Practice compassion. Surrender to spirit. Only your Higher Power is in control. Live in the eternal here and now, and learn to Live Yes.

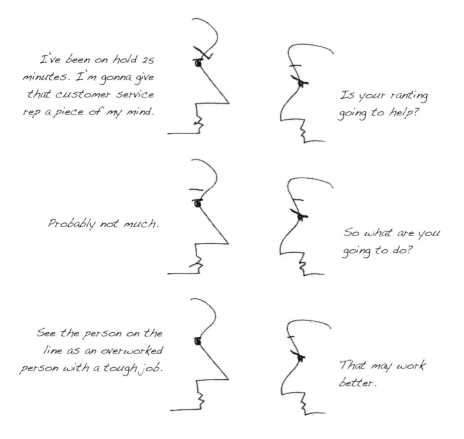

THE ANNOYED-WORRY CYCLE

Break the pattern with acceptance.

Imagine that someone says something you don't like. You get annoyed. Then you think about what that person meant, and you worry. The worry annoys you more. You get more tense. You tighten. As you judge, you stay annoyed. Your mind keeps finding something else to worry about or get annoyed with. And you go back and forth between annoyance and worry.

My brother leaves me a message that he has to talk about our mother. I call my brother's cell phone. No answer. I call his wife's cell phone. No answer. I call my mother's home and her cell phone. It's Sunday night, and everyone should be home. No answer. I begin to build a giant worry story about how they're all in the emergency room talking to the doctor and can't answer their phones. I call him again, he answers and says there's no crisis, and also asks why I worry so much. I am annoyed that he didn't call me back since he knew I was upset. I worry that he'll do it again. I become more annoyed as I think of the other times I thought he ignored my feelings. After all this, I can't sleep. The sad thing is that *nothing happened*. I created this annoyance and worry in my own head — for nothing.

Annoyance is focusing on the past. Worry is focusing on the future. We keep jumping from past to future and from future to past, back and forth, over and over. Nowhere are we in the here and now. Nowhere are we using the present moment to forget about the past or ignore the unknown future. Nowhere are we practicing the gift of mindfulness.

Let's get off the treadmill of looking backward and forward and start to notice where we are. Within the chaos of useless beliefs and troubling emotions is an opportunity to create a new pattern. By framing each experience in the moment and not getting stuck in the past or worried about the future, we can live a life that is closer to our hopes and farther from our past habits.

Living Yes gives us an opportunity to reduce our anxiety by getting to its cause. It calls us to accept whatever happens. Acceptance doesn't mean giving up. It means finding a way to work with the truth. Living Yes calls for us to say "Yes" to reality even when it scares the pee out of us, because that's what's being offered.

Being brave requires taking a stand. Going into battle does not require us to be fearless. Going into battle without any fear would be reckless. Instead we take a battle stance. Even on wobbly legs, we put one foot in front of the other and move forward. Courage does not require us to be a cartoon hero. Courage gives us an opportunity to say "Yes" to whatever Life has to offer. We don't have to be stronger, more perfect, or holier than we already are. We just march, feel, or think. Let us raise our inner hero and seek the truth through a process of Living Yes.

EXERCISE—USING SEPARATING EMOTIONS TO CHANGE YOUR THINKING   ☒

You can use separating emotions to identify how you are thinking "No." From there you may reverse yourself and Live Yes. Here are some patterns that you can use to work back from your feelings to the thoughts that started them. Begin by identifying the emotion. Then select the closest No. Your lesson may be found in the form of the Yes response.

Anger (annoyance, irritation, rage)

External / Relational

NO	YES
Judging others, not accepting.	Forgiving. Accepting humanity. (Humanity is the knowledge that as humans we have limits.)
Blaming others.	Forgiving. Taking responsibility.
Not tolerating others.	Being humble. Being human.
Being abandoned or ignored by others.	Allowing limits, being human. I know the universe is kind.
Violated boundary.	Identity. I know who I am, and what I will tolerate.

Anger (annoyance, irritation, rage)

Internal / Personal

NO	YES
Blame, intolerance, harmful judgment of self, resentment.	Humility. Humanity.
Demanding to change the past.	Accepting.
Demanding to know.	Accepting.
Not able to accomplish a goal.	Accepting limits. Being human and capable.
I don't get what I want; my life is harder than everyone else's.	I am human. I am lovable. I experience gratitude.
Violated boundary.	Identity. I know who I am, and what I will tolerate.

Anxiety (worry, apprehension, fear, dread)

External / Relational

NO	YES
Danger from situations.	Surrendering to Higher Power. Faithful. Present.
Danger from others.	Capable of acting safely and setting boundaries. Human. Faithful. Present.

Anxiety (worry, apprehension, fear, dread)

Internal / Personal

NO	YES
Fixated on your own limits. Frozen by risk.	Humility. Accepting your humanity.
Stuck in past traumas.	Freedom. Faith that the present is infinite. Free will. Spiritual healing.
Can't do what I expect.	Accepting. Can't know the future. I do my best.
Overwhelmed.	Grateful. Faithful.
Not trusting spirit.	Faith.

Sadness (grief, depression, heartbreak)

External / Relational

NO	YES
I cannot recover what's lost, and I'm lost without it.	Getting out of the past. Accepting. Not my fault. Compassion.
Irresolvable issue.	Accepting. Humble. Allowing limits. Humanity.
The world is a crazy, messed-up place.	Acceptance. Compassion.
Disconnecting. No one understands me.	Faith.

Sadness (grief, depression, heartbreak)

Internal / Personal

NO	YES
Lonely. Indulgent. No one loves me. I'm not lovable.	Faith. Knowledge that the universe / self / others love me. Discipline. Unselfishness.
What I value is lost. I am adrift without an anchor.	Self-awareness of what I have. Gratitude. Faith.

Disgust (revulsion)

External / Relational

NO	YES
I have to pretend I'm more than I am.	Humility.

Disgust (revulsion)

Internal / Personal

NO	YES
Trapped by past traumas.	Freedom. Faith that the present is infinite. Free will. Spiritual healing.
Harsh self-judgment. Loser!	Acceptance. There is enough love for me. Being human.
Intolerant of reality.	Accepting.
Production failure (unmet expectations).	Nothing's perfect. Zero expectations.

Boredom (apathy, ennui)

External / Relational

NO	YES
Disconnected.	Faith.
Hopeless.	Peace, freedom. Faith.

Boredom (apathy, ennui)

Internal / Personal

NO	YES
Low energy.	I don't control everything. "Let go and let God."
Blocked imagination.	Freedom.
Tired.	Rest. Relax. Take time for myself.
Not interested.	Allow for the best in others. Unselfish. Human.

Shame (embarrassed, humiliation)

External / Relational

NO	YES
I'm not loved.	Faith. I am lovable. I love myself.
I have to blame others.	I take full responsibility and, once done, I forgive others.
Stuck in the past.	Forgive others. Accept change.

Shame (embarrassed, humiliation)

Internal / Personal

NO	YES
I'm inadequate, worthless, stupid.	I'm the creation of the universe. I can love, so I am loveable.
I don't know who I am.	I am who I am.
I have too many flaws.	I am human.
I have to blame myself.	I take full responsibility and, once done, I forgive myself.
Self-judgment.	Self-forgiveness.
It's about me.	It's not about me. Forgiveness. Humility. Humanity.

Confusion

External / Relational

NO	YES
I cannot find my personal power.	Faith in who I am.
I do not know my place in the world or what is real.	Faith that things are as they should be. I'm here to learn from this.
Too much going on.	Examine false belief. Acceptance.
Trapped by negative people or negative situation.	Evaluate limits. No demands of perfection.

Confusion

Internal / Personal

NO	YES
I don't know who I am.	I am a child of the universe. I'm a human, and I do the best I can.
I am separated from Spirit.	Faith in what is.
Demanding to know outcome.	Accepting. Humanity.

BEING AND DOING NO

You struggle to prove to the world that you're okay.

When we believe the No, we attack ourselves. When we believe the No, our reactive mind grabs us by the throat and pulls us down. No wonder being stuck in No feels like hell! And we get caught in a feedback loop.

Here's how the loop works: When you believe your reactive mind, you are believing that you are flawed, broken, unworthy, incapable, unimportant, or weak. You do something to defend or prove your core lie is false. That seems natural, but the way you do this is not honest. Instead of rejecting the No by taking a stand that you are human, whole, worthy, capable, important, strong, and honest, you cover up or defend the horrifying lie that you are telling yourself. You hide the No with avoidance, judgment, anxiety, anger, and other self-destructive methods of denying your true *being*. You buy in to your core lies. And because of that, you think you have to *do* something to prove yourself. When you act to mask those lies, you invest more strongly in the idea that your core lies are true.

You create a list of what you have to do to prove the lie

is untrue. That requires pretending. There is a loop that forms when you behave based on your core lies or your truths. It works like this: I am (being) _selfish_, so I have to (do) _something to prove I'm not selfish_.

And when you start pretending (covering up the core lie), you go back to believing other Noes about yourself (accusing yourself of a core lie). As you believe new accusations, you make up things to do to prove them wrong. You find yourself moving from Being No to Doing No, back to Being No, back to Doing No. And this goes on and on in an unending, downward cycle. Both are traps. Both are ways to say "No" to the world.

Chart – The Looping Trap (Vicious Cycle)

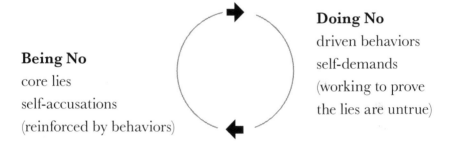

Being No
core lies
self-accusations
(reinforced by behaviors)

Doing No
driven behaviors
self-demands
(working to prove
the lies are untrue)

Being No includes a list of core lies and self-accusations (such as "liar, inadequate, unimportant") that you use to accuse yourself. Doing No includes the burdens of driven behaviors and demands you put on yourself in order to prove to others that the core lies are untrue.

It works differently for each person, usually focusing on one or two core lies and different ways to cover them with driven behaviors. Look at the chart that follows, and notice which words come up strongest for you. Then rewrite a version that shows how your personal loop works.

Chart— *The Loop of Core Lies (Accusations) and Driven Behaviors (Demands)*

...I accuse myself of being...
a liar
...so I think I have to...
manipulate, and because I manipulate
...I accuse myself of being...
inadequate
...so I think I have to...
be perfect, and because I'm not perfect
...I accuse myself of being...
even more inadequate
...so I think I have to...
pretend, but that feels fake, and
...I accuse myself of being...
weak
...so I think I have to...
be special, but people don't treat me as special, so
...I accuse myself of being...
foolish and stupid
...so I think I have to...

show how smart I am, but that is a burden, which separates me from others and so
...I accuse myself of being...
unimportant
...so I think I have to...
be the center of attention, and because that doesn't work...
...I accuse myself of being...
alone
...so I think I have to...
be everybody's friend, a big pleaser, and because people don't like that so much
...I accuse myself of being...
broken
...so I think I have to...
hide out and isolate, and because that leaves me alone
...I accuse myself of being...
unlovable
...so I think I have to...
prove myself by being thin, sexy, healthy, but I don't prove myself, so
...I accuse myself of being...
weak

...so I think I have to...

be better than everyone else, so I drive myself and suffer, and

...I accuse myself of being...

worthless

...so I think I have to...

prove myself, but I become so driven and competitive that I feel hollow, and

...I accuse myself of being...

unable to feel and less than human

...so I think I have to...

get loaded, but the demand is too heavy, because

...I accuse myself of being...

unlovable

...so I think I have to...

hide the lies, manipulate, and deceive,

and I continue in this unending loop, this cycle of No and fake proving, on and on, in a way that is uniquely me, until...

I learn to Live Yes. And discover who I really am.

CREATIVE LOOPING

Find the truth loop.

You can create a constructive loop. When you believe you are capable, you interpret what happens based on your personal strength. This helps you believe in your own abilities. You can create an upward cycle. Go back to the core lie and recognize how you are saying "No." Use the Living Yes skills to take a stand on the truth. Create a loop based on that truth.

Chart – The Truth Loop (Virtuous Cycle)

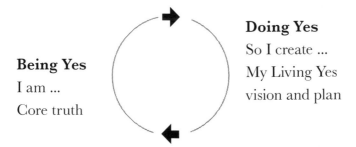

Being Yes
I am ...
Core truth

Doing Yes
So I create ...
My Living Yes
vision and plan

For example, instead of having to manipulate because you think you are unlovable, do what a lovable and loving person would do. Living Yes will reinforce your self-esteem.

EXERCISE—CREATE A TRUTH LOOP   ☒

Use the alternative thoughts that you began to develop in Chapter Four, and create a truth loop. Be sure that you put some core truths on the left side and some creative actions on the right side.

PROGRESS CHECK

What is the difference between anger management and anger prevention?

What strategies do you find work best for each?

Where in your life are you making efforts to control others? How does this increase your anxiety?

What methods do you use to break the downward cycle of anger and worry?

Who are some of the people in your life who deserve more compassion?

Answer these questions about your personal core lies again: What are the most common core lies that you tell yourself when you are under stress?

What is the opposite core truth?

Do you struggle to meet imagined demands by proving yourself? How can you reverse this?

What have you learned by creating a truth loop? How has your personal loop changed since you wrote it?

Patterns of No

AVOIDANCE – DIVIDE AND CONQUER NOTHING

Avoidance is a short-term strategy that fails over time.

Any behavior will be a choice between Yes or No. We approach or we avoid. Approach is confident action, problem solving, stepping forward even when afraid, complete acceptance, Living Yes. Approach behavior follows the three A's: Acknowledgement, Acceptance, and Action.

The opposite, avoidance, is withdrawing, being passive, falling victim, seeing only your own suffering, indulging, anger, anxiety, making efforts to control Life, depression, saying "No." Avoidance is a failed attempt to control your environment. By running away or hiding from reality, you are denying the truth. You are saying "No" to Life. Withdrawing from your pain is giving in to your pain. Avoidance is a short-term control strategy. It may work for a little while, but in time it will come back to bite you.

Approach is the goal, an intentional and fully aware engagement with the situation. When an airline pilot comes toward the runway for landing, he must approach with all of his intention and concentration. He keeps his eyes on the engine gauges and out the window, and communicates with the tower, the crew, and the passengers. He pulls back on the throttle, drops the flaps, keeps the plane level and knows how far it is to the ground. All of this is required to land safely. He cannot avoid any part of the landing or the consequences could be horrible. Live Yes as if you are landing a plane. Avoidance is rarely the best option.

The pilot's successful landing approach is fully focused and engaged. Once committed, he is unlikely to feel self-indulgent or distressed. A professional pilot will fully execute each part of his landing. His emotions and thoughts are in service to the important task of landing the plane. Just like the pilot, your behavior can determine how you feel.

It's the same for a professional athlete on game day. And so it is for us every day. Live Yes by keeping your "eyes on the prize." This reduces, delays, or bypasses any unmanageable depression or anxiety.

We have a false belief that if we avoid discomfort, we will escape the pain altogether. Unfortunately, this does not work. The more we avoid, the more we suffer. As we avoid a challenging situation, our emotions grow more anxious, more depressed, and more separated. Then we work even harder to avoid, which makes us more anxious, afraid, depressed, unhappy, and separated. So we avoid more, feel separated more, and on and on. The downward cycle continues as we dig ourselves into deeper and deeper patterns of avoidance and withdrawal.

Avoidance does not work in the long term. Abusing drugs and alcohol is a tempting avoidance strategy that fails in time. Too much gambling, purchasing, eating, and lust are tempting avoidance strategies that fail in time. Out-of-control rage, indulging your fears, and saying "No" to everything are tempting avoidance strategies that fail in time. If you do not wisely manage your physical sense pleasures and your emotional urges, you can become overloaded and lose your purpose. Instead, Live Yes with discipline and vision. (More is written about seeking pleasure in Chapter Nine.)

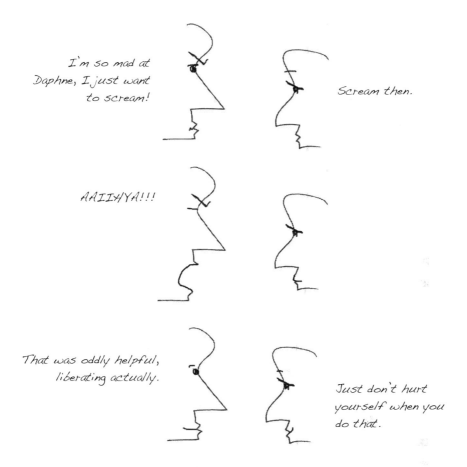

BALANCING USEFUL AVOIDANCE

Avoidance is measured by intention.

Sometimes it is not obvious whether our behaviors are closer to approach or avoidance. Leaving the scene instead of confronting somebody could be seen as a way to avoid the discomfort of standing up to a bully, or it may be a way for you to chill, relax, and regroup. Watching television may be a way to avoid the world and numb out, or watching television might be a way to enjoy yourself. It depends on what you intend. If you approach with a clear idea of what you want to do (watch my favorite sitcom), you are Living Yes. But if you are tuning

out and avoiding unpleasant emotions through distraction
(turn on the tube and get away from this), you are choosing No
by avoiding.

The cost of avoiding your experience is giving up your life.
You can say "No" by hiding from thoughts that are upsetting
or avoiding emotions that cause pain. Avoidance often becomes
unconscious until you later become overwhelmed by consequences. By saying "No" in this way you rob yourself of your
strength and your ability to overcome obstacles that are in your
path.

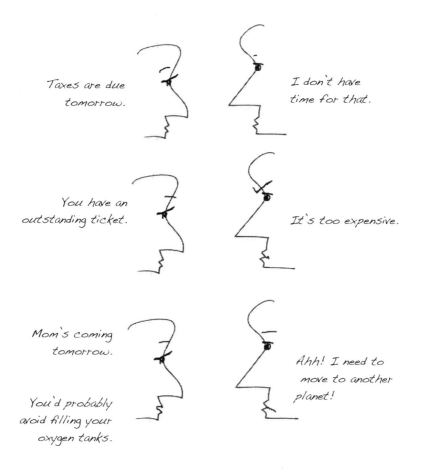

PTSD

Post-traumatic stress is the No of avoidance.

Many people who are sexually abused as children and many, such as combat veterans, who experienced frightening near-death experiences, have developed a complicated avoidance strategy that psychologists call PTSD, which stands for Post Traumatic Stress Disorder. PTSD is what happens when your shock prevents you from dealing with your pain. Part of the definition of PTSD is "persistent avoidance of stimuli associated with the trauma." Said another way, PTSD is hiding from a past painful moment that you cannot process. When anything reminds you of the painful moment, you return to that place of horror, so you bury and avoid it. You never got a chance to file those scary thoughts into memory, so they rise quickly. A car backfires, and you think it's a bomb. Someone is walking behind you, and you feel frightened. The memory is being triggered. Until you can stop avoiding the horrible truth that you once faced and say "Yes" to the safety you have now, you will remain shocked, sad, and helpless. The avoidance served you well at the time, but now, many years later, it's time to Live Yes and let it go.

I had another drowning nightmare last night.

What did you do?

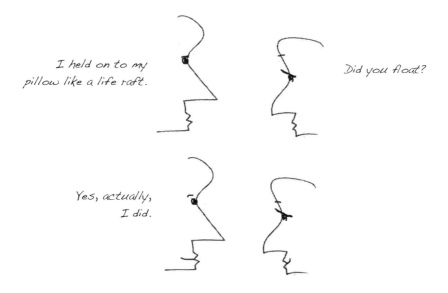

~~~~~~

EXERCISE — CHANGING FROM NO TO YES
USING THE FIVE PRACTICES: *Notices, Faith, Knowledge,*
Action, and Continuing Gratitude   ☒
~~~~~~

This exercise offers a path to Live Yes. By bringing your mind
through these five stages, you will be able to get to No quickly
(Notices), open yourself to imagine new ideas (Faith), use your
powerful mind (Knowledge), engage life (Action), and remain
connected to spirit (Continuing Gratitude).

1. Notices — Notice when you are saying *NO* to *T*ruth *in*
*C*ognition, *E*motion, and *S*ensation. Notice specific triggers
and how you respond with thoughts, feelings, and body sensations. Use the techniques from Chapter Five. Breathe. "One
day at a time." Your problems are not the same as you. Identify
and move past false, secondary gains. Seek mercy.

2. Faith — Believe in unseen possibility. There is a way past worry and doubt. Recognize that you can be the biggest threat to your own success. Big solutions (quantum, exponential) have more energy than smaller problems (Newtonian, addition). Hope overcomes despair. How might this incident be seen as a gift from the universe? "Let go and let God." Accept. Is it possible that your No could be Yes? Seek inner spirit to guide you to Truth. Find Grace.

3. Knowledge — Use insight and experience. Be willing to move past fear and perceived catastrophe. Cognitive theory (Chapter Five). Give up "stinkin' thinkin'." Choose to connect rather than separate. Take a stand on the Truth that comes from your values. Esteem. Be confident. Envision a new approach; imagine exciting new outcomes. Offer and receive love with clear intentions. Feel gratitude. "An attitude of gratitude."

4. Action — Make choices as a wise warrior. Walk a "hero's walk" by moving forward with wobbly steps. Be willing to "take the licks." If you fall, get up and keep going. "Fall seven times, stand up eight." Keep focus. "Faith without works is dead." Test your beliefs scientifically. Make up experiments. Consult objective experts and writings. Use support wisely. Be thankful for any change. Learn humility.

5. Continuing Gratitude — Reverence, honor, connection, peace, love. Re-live the upward cycle of beneficial changes. Go back to "Notices," and begin the process again with expanded faith, knowledge, capacity for courageous and continuous action, and gratitude.

JUDGMENT

Judgment is not your job.

You may notice that you mentally attack yourself or others. This angry behavior comes from making a Big Judgment. When you demand to be right, you are trapped at every turn. Those Big Judgments are revealed by the way you talk. Every time you hear yourself say that you or others "should" behave in a certain way or "have to" behave in a certain way, you are unleashing your Big Judgment.

Big Judgments occur when you are faking that you are bigger than you actually are. Sometimes judgment is such a large idea that it is useful to leave it to your Higher Power. Be clear about the difference between a healthful evaluation and a Big Judgment by looking at the context and the usefulness of the thought. Any label or accusation, such as judging yourself or others with a core lie, calls for a bigger context than one person may have.

Many core lies start with that type of Big Judgment thinking. "I'm inadequate, stupid, weak, not good enough, hopeless, and helpless" are examples of core lies that are judgments taken out of context. It is not useful to pretend that you are all-knowing, especially when the result is a core lie about yourself or others.

Before jumping into judgment about all this judgment, let's get our terms straight. There is a difference between making a choice ("I'll wear the black pants today"), offering an insight ("I believe that you are hurting yourself with your drinking"), evaluating a situation ("I like this house, but it won't work for my disabled child"), and making a Big Judgment ("You are a loser"). Sometimes they overlap, but only the Big Judgment is rooted in a lie. Only the Big Judgment lacks benefit. Only the Big Judgment can cause harm.

Attaching to judgments is a way that you believe you can ease the core lies that you tell yourself. Believing those judgments leads you to struggle to prove that your lies are wrong by creating a false self. The self-righteous bigot appears to himself to be better than the victim, but his efforts are to prove himself worthy, adequate, strong, or smart. He is using judgment to fight his own doubts, and he is doing this by claiming a bigger context than his own limitations of being one individual human.

Chart – Big Judgment Words List

Below is a list of judging phrases. None of these do you any good. Stop using these **No** words.

SELF-JUDGING WORDS	JUDGING WORDS
I should	You should
I'm supposed to	You're supposed to
I have to	You have to
I've got to	You've got to
I must	You must
I need to	You need to
I ought to	You ought to
I can't	You can't
Self-criticism	Criticizing others
I'm "right"	You're "right"
I'm "wrong"	You're "wrong"
I'm "good"	You're "good'
I'm "bad"	You're "bad"
Judge	Judge
Demand	Demand

Judgment is condemnation after unmet expectations. Having zero expectations will prevent you from having anything to judge. This is why expectations were discussed early, in Chapter One.

As you continue to make harsh demands on yourself, you reinforce your core lies (worthless, unlovable, useless, weak, stupid). And as you play that losing game, you dig in and hurt yourself some more. You think you are forcing yourself to become the opposite of your core lies (worthy, useful, strong, smart). You think you are whipping yourself into shape, but you are only making things worse. Instead, you might choose to find a way to allow the gift of Living Yes to come into your life.

The honest truth comes from Living Yes. You cannot Live Yes and prove your core lies are wrong by pretending that you are as powerful as "God." That is "ego" behavior. Instead, Live Yes by allowing yourself to be a vulnerable, human, open-hearted, and flawed being. If you approach your life this way, you will find that Big Judgments are unnecessary.

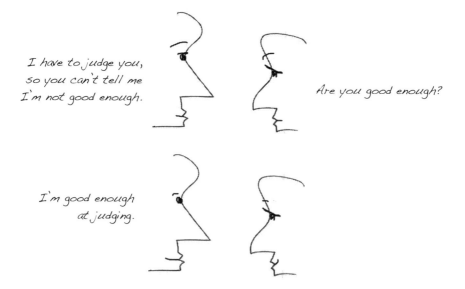

I have to judge you, so you can't tell me I'm not good enough.

Are you good enough?

I'm good enough at judging.

HABITS, STUCK IN ME

Habits may trap you into blind pathways.

Habits are shortcuts we have learned that allow our brain to repeat tasks without using much thinking space. When learning to tie our shoelaces, we train our fingers to follow a complex set of instructions. Once mastered, we tie our shoes without thinking, so we may use our mind to create new abilities.

Habits become a problem when they are not in service to our best nature. We develop those so-called "bad habits" in our brains where they were once used for something we thought was "good." Perhaps you smoked your first cigarette to feel cool, or to relax, or to experiment, but now those old benefits are lost in a pattern of psychological and physical addiction. Beginning with what appeared to be positive, you are now doing something destructive.

As you practice a habit, you get deeper into it as a pattern. "Practice makes permanent." Unfortunately, some habits are no longer helpful for the situation. The pathways in your brain dig grooves deeper and deeper, like car tracks on a dirt road. Simply saying "No" does not always stop those habits because the pattern has been too deeply dug in. Get out of the rut by finding a positive behavior that you can substitute for the destructive behavior. For example: Replace cigarettes with gum. Replace watching TV with exercise. Replace eating food by playing outside with the kids or the dog.

One helpful way to meet your commitments is with ritual. If you do the same action at the same time in the same way in a repeated manner, you will gain the power of the ritual. Ritual deepens the activation of intentional habits, growth, and rewards. It also deepens habit patterns in the brain.

SECONDARY GAIN

We miss the Yes because of false payoffs.

Sometimes it is helpful to look at the false benefits that we use to maintain bad habits. This is called "secondary gain." Secondary gain is a (false) payoff that leads you to do something that on the surface is self-destructive. You may be continuing a bad habit to show yourself you don't have to change. You may be trying to prove yourself right by making others wrong. You may be playing the victim, so everyone will take care of you.

The way to identify your secondary gain is to look for what type of (false) payoff you think you are getting from a destructive activity. Ask yourself, "What would I lose if I got better?" You'll find yourself believing a core lie about yourself. You'll find some part of you is getting to be right or righteous with a cost that is greater than you can see.

Perhaps you lie so you won't have to face disappointment, hurt, or anger. Perhaps you avoid so you don't have to face something unpleasant. Perhaps you cannot tolerate your own tears. Sometimes you don't make an effort, so you have a pre-made excuse for failure. But this only works for a moment, and then you're still stuck in your No.

Perhaps as a little girl, your mother yelled at you every time you were late for the school bus. You learned to make excuses, blame others, and point to circumstances beyond your control. After that, perhaps she would forgive you. You were learning that lying would keep someone from becoming angry with you. As you got older, you practiced the same habit, lying to avoid confronting your boss or spouse. A habit of lying set in.

Your secondary gain for lying was that you could avoid having others become angry at you. Because of your avoiding lies and hiding skills, you did not develop the ability to face people who were confronting you. In time, your lies and habit structure became automatic and powerful. The habit of lying has been a big No. You have been selling yourself out for a secondary gain.

Instead, learn to follow your intuition rather than your judgment. Move from head to heart. Stop believing your core lies and Live Yes from your honest, human self.

Unless you are willing to risk hurting someone you love, you cannot tell him or her the truth. If you lie about not having back pain so your mother doesn't worry, that's a secondary gain. It will backfire when she doesn't understand why you can't move the couch or why you are so easily irritated. From there your resentment is likely to build.

But by accepting life on Life's terms, you do not take responsibility for your mother's feelings, and you may honor and love her enough to trust her with the truth. This is not permission to indulge, gossip, or complain. It is a guidepost toward finding the truth and living your full-out Yes in the situation.

Sometimes the lesson is to accept that being honest may hurt others. If you can overcome your fear but remain compassionate, you may find yourself more willing to tell the truth to others and to yourself. Practice telling others difficult truths with compassion. Reject your secondary gain and stand on your Yes of the situation. You will no longer have to depend on the habit. This works for all habits, including addictions.

~~~~~~
EXERCISE – THE SECONDARY GAIN PROCESS   ⊠
~~~~~~

1. Identify a habit you don't like.

2. Identify the secondary gain (false benefit).

3. Fulfill that gain in other ways.

4. Let go of the destructive behavior. If there is a useful task or helpful behavior that you don't do, take a step toward doing it.

5. Seek support. (More is written about support in Chapter Eight.)

Some pointers: Be conscious. Be compassionate. Start with small steps. Start with brief commitments.

~~~~~~

If you have what seems like a crazy thought which triggers you to behave in a way that is self-destructive, consider the possibility that part of you believes the crazy thought. *Then,* do the opposite. Noticing secondary gain is a great way to catch yourself in such patterns as destructive thinking, social phobia, co-dependence, and avoiding emotions.

The secondary gain for social phobia involves a false way to avoid other people's judgments. When you are not depending on their judgments, you will become more able to create a self that can Live Yes no matter what others do.

The secondary gain for co-dependence involves a false way to believe you are useful or connected. As we discussed in Chapter Three, you do not have to enable or rescue in order to be important.

The secondary gain for avoiding uncomfortable feelings or thoughts is a false sense of protection. The cost is that you don't get to be a feeling person. If it's sadness you avoid, find a situation to generate sadness. If it's anger you don't express freely, find a situation where you may safely express anger. If hiding gives you a false sense of calm, expose yourself to whatever makes you emotionally exposed.

You may be surprised at the power and freedom you discover when you do this process. Our minds tend to make situations much worse than they play out in reality. Act in the service of Living Yes, and you will find freedom.

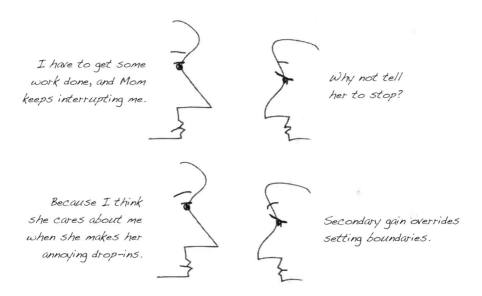

I have to get some work done, and Mom keeps interrupting me.

Why not tell her to stop?

Because I think she cares about me when she makes her annoying drop-ins.

Secondary gain overrides setting boundaries.

EXERCISE—TWO-COLUMN COST/BENEFIT PROCESS ⊠

Run a "cost/benefit" analysis of a problem habit.

1. Make a list of the costs.
2. Make a list of the benefits.
3. Compare.
4. Change.

Identify a problem habit and write it on the top of the page.
Below that, make two columns. On the left write the costs to
you of the habit. On the right write the benefits.

1. You can probably identify the costs easily. For example,
consider the bad habit of lying. You may find that you are
not able to be honest with others, not be able to be who you
really are, think you have to stay consistent and remember
the lies, feel shame at having been exposed for lying. Write
the costs.

2. Examine the benefits column. The key is to identify the
false benefit. How is the benefit an illusion? For example,
with the lying habit, you may get short-term advantages of
not being judged or yelled at. The psychological benefit is
illusion. You may get someone to think you're special for a while.
The benefit may be something you have not yet considered.
Those benefits are the "secondary gains" just described, and
examining them closely can be an insightful way to find the
obstacles to changing your habit.

3. Now review the columns. Remember that the benefits
are false or temporary. You have lost your freedom if you
cannot choose to behave outside the habit. The habit is not
serving you.

4. The final step is to change your behavior. Choose an action
and do it. If something is holding you back, do the secondary
gain process that was just described, including support.

~~~~~~

Let's look at how this process might work with the problem
of refusing to quit smoking. The costs might be your health, the

bad smells, your reputation, and your physical addiction. The primary gain would be that the nicotine relaxes you. The secondary (false) gain would be that you don't have to face your weakness.

Let's look at how this process might work for putting off cutting the grass. The cost might be an unkempt lawn, can't find the morning paper, people throwing trash in your yard, angry neighbors, feeling shame. The primary gains include not having to sweat, or getting to sit on the couch for hours. The secondary (false) gain might be getting to keep the neighbors from asking you favors, and getting attention from the entire neighborhood.

When you look at your behaviors, including the costs and the secondary gains, it should be clear that they are keeping you in a No. This is a challenging exercise, but a change in habit is essential if you want to Live Yes.

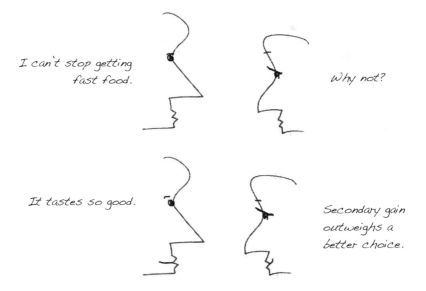

PROGRESS CHECK

Where have you used avoidance to soothe yourself in the past?

Have you been able to admit areas where you are avoiding challenges that you had not noticed before?

How have you changed from No to Yes in your life? Where can you apply the five practices of Notices, Faith, Knowledge, Action, and Continuing Gratitude?

Have you noticed where in your life you are judging yourself or others?

Can you give an example from your life of the difference between making a Big Judgment and a useful choice?

Have you noticed where in your life you use judgment words? How often do you use them?

What areas of potential change do you miss because of secondary gain? What are you doing to correct that?

Where have you added healthful behaviors in place of habits you wish to correct?

Some Practical Ideas

THE PAIN BLAME

If we cannot tolerate our discomfort, we will make reactive choices.

Society offers us a failed technique to react to long-term physical pain; namely, suck it up and quit whining. Unfortunately, it doesn't work. The endure-it-with-toughness approach can hammer us until we break. And if we can't take it, we're seen as a "weakling" reacting to every little scratch. We live in a society that is stuck in No toward pain.

Emotional and physical pain are part of our lives. When we feel heat from the flame, we quickly withdraw our hands to avoid getting burned. Pain gives us a guidepost for how to protect our bodies. Life has pain built in, starting with the fire of conception. We create our own bodies, 1 cell, 2 cells, 4 cells, 8 cells, 16 cells. And we push through pain to draw our first breath.

The idea of overcoming pain in order to evolve is a deep part of our character. Emotional pain shows us where to grow stronger. Suffering is a deeply human experience. Suffering provides a necessary resistance. We sometimes hear "God never gives us a burden greater than we can handle." Life is designed to include pain. If we did not experience pain, we would not choose to limit ourselves. We would have no reason to find useful boundaries. Accepting pain is another way to Live Yes.

Overcoming obstacles by standing on our highest principles has been in our stories for thousands of years. In mythology, the hero journeys through many painful experiences. In almost every movie, the lead actor or actors must apply some higher principles to overcome physical or emotional problems. An ancient saying goes "The obstacle is the path," and perhaps we can add the idea that "The path is the obstacle."

Sometimes, we must experience intense pain in the short term in order to help us get stronger over time. For example, taking an injection or drinking a miserable-tasting medicine to clear your illness is a way to Live Yes through pain. Of course, chronic pain that may not go away easily can challenge your ability to Live Yes daily.

As you know, how you think determines how you feel. Pain is not the problem, although it is certainly real. How you interpret the pain is the problem. How you act while in pain is the true test. Accept that pain is another of Life's unwanted gifts. Just as with all the events that you resist in your life, pain offers opportunities to deepen your ability to be a vulnerable human.

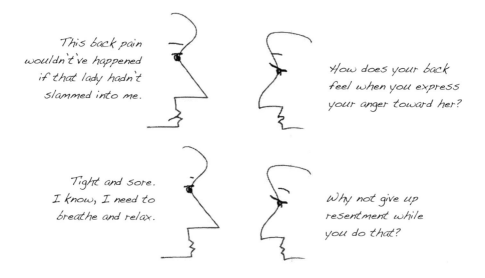

The signals that tell you that you are hurting are part of Life's gift. Sometimes it is difficult but important to accept that you cannot be free of all pain. Avoiding pain makes pain worse.

Accepting or even embracing pain, rather than avoiding pain, is the way to Live Yes. What you choose to do with pain is what matters. The thoughts of the present moment are the only truth. If that means fully embracing physical pain, then that is the choice that Reality is inviting you to make.

EXERCISE — WHOLE BODY PAIN PROCESS ☒

Find a place in your body that does not hurt. Perhaps it is as small as a spot on your leg, a fingertip, or a single cell. Put all your attention on the spot and begin to breathe, slowly and rhythmically. Imagine the pain-free area is growing. Don't push faster than it wants to go. Keep your attention on the area without pain. Keep breathing. Keep expanding slowly. You may be surprised at how you improve.

FATE VERSUS DESTINY, FREE WILL

You are not your culture, family, or belief system. Infinite possibilities and opportunities are here for you right here, right now.

Let's define *fate* as what is given to us, and let's define *destiny* as what we make of it. Unfortunately, many of us think we are trapped by fate. To live in a fate trap is to live in a world with no freedom and no ability to make changes. In that world filled with No, fate is a hopeless, changeless hell.

When we believe in the fate trap, everything seems to say "No." We see a world filled with negative signs. The daily newspaper is full of "No." People band together in fear of outsiders. Right versus left. Rich versus poor. Young versus old. Us versus them. Mine versus yours. Fear versus reason. No versus bigger No.

Fated to be trapped, our No grows. People use labels against one another. Everyone is angry and flawed. Parents are scaring and scarring their children. A powerful drive to protect us from evils that may or may not exist moves anger to hate. Standing on shaky ground of having to protect ourselves, our fears grow. From fear, greed grows.

Fate traps take over our communities. Sects of religions are formed from beliefs in small gods, including the failings of other societies' religious practices. Themes emerge, based on science over spirit or spirit over science. Armies are raised for various reasons, and then humans violently destroy one another.

Are we fated to live in this trapped world of No? Can we take initiative, claim our destiny, and Live Yes one piece at a time? One peace at a time?

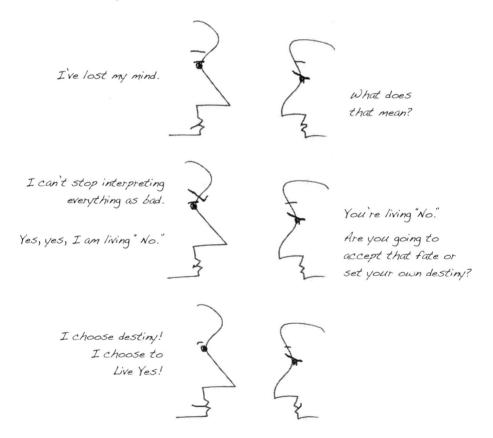

When was the first time you stopped living in the world you were taught to live in? Were you a teenage rebel who broke away from your father's rules (like James Dean in the classic film *Rebel without a Cause*)? Were you an upstart youngster who pursued art or a sport despite your parents' fears? Did you go with the crowd or stand up to it? Think a moment. When was your first original thought? And was that thought one where you decided to do something special, something new, something only you could do? (And if you haven't done it yet, maybe it's time to do it now!) George Carlin pointed out that "Those who dance are considered insane by those who can't hear the music." Find your music and live your destiny.

You have had opportunities to make a choice beyond your fate, beyond what was expected and restricted for you. This is not news. When you express your free will, you set a new pattern for your future. You overcome your limited fate and express and experience your destiny. This is the moment when you first taste the idea of Living Yes.

"Be yourself; everyone else is already taken." You are no good to others or to yourself if you do not claim your power. That power comes from using your knowledge, following your intuition, and Living Yes toward your own destiny.

While reading this section, did you began thinking about breaking free of your fate, identifying your destiny, and making a plan to take action? If so, you are ready to put pen to paper and claim your destiny.

~~~~~~
EXERCISE — BREAKING FREE, DESTINY IN ACTION   ⊠
~~~~~~

Identify your childhood values. What were you taught when you were growing up? What were the spoken and unspoken rules? What behaviors were expected in order to fit in? What judgments were taught, especially about outsiders? (Examine family, community, culture, nationality, media influence, and world civilization.)

Close your eyes and float back in time. Identify three ways you followed those values.

Come back to the present. Pick two times you went against or beyond those values. That is, when did you do something no one, including you — especially you — expected or predicted you would do?

Close your eyes and float back in time. Remember as far back as you can to a time when you went against those values and did something unexpected. See if you can identify the first time. That is when you began to live out your destiny.

~~~~~~
EXERCISE — FATE OR DESTINY   ⊠
~~~~~~

Write a "fate" story. What would you be doing today if you had not broken free? If instead you had followed your fate, where would you be? How would you think?

Review how you overcame your fate, and write a phrase that defines your destiny. Include the context of how you act toward others.

Write a "destiny" story. What and where will you be in five years as you continue to follow your destiny?

~~~~~~

PUTTING TRUTH INTO ACTION

Take concrete steps to Live Yes.

Once you have examined your life and identified your destiny, you can put this truth into action. The most common planning tool is to identify your mission, goals, and objectives. This is how businesses set their course and identify each step in moving forward. You can do the same with your life.

A mission statement is a power-packed phrase that acts as a guiding principle. This is the focus of who you are and where you are heading. It shows the path of how you will Live Yes. Here are three examples of mission statements: "Constantly work to uplift my mood and those around me." "Support myself and others in following my spiritual principles." "Keep myself mentally fresh and physically strong."

It takes time and practice to develop a powerful and centered mission statement. The work you just completed about moving from fate to destiny is a good way to begin. Once a genuine mission statement is created, you can move on to goals and objectives. In modern business language, goals are broad areas you want to accomplish, and objectives are the measurable actions you take to arrive at your goals. They might look like this:

Mission Statement: Constantly work to uplift my mood and be kinder to those around me.

Goal: Be proactive to improve my mood.

    Objective: Study uplifting books at least one time per week.

    Objective: Process thought records daily.

    Objective: Smile daily.

    Objective: Socialize every weekend.

    Objective: Eat well, exercise, and sleep regularly.

Objective: Read over The Living Yes Principles daily.

Objective: Read the *Living Yes* book three times.

Objective: Every hour examine whether I am Living Yes or stuck in No.

Goal: Help others

Objective: Attend community events.

Objective: Give to a charity.

Objective: Smile each day to a stranger.

Objective: Say something kind to my partner each morning.

Objective: Express my gratitude to all those who are serving me.

EXERCISE – PLANNING TOOLS   ⊠

Here are instructions for applying these ideas:

Mission: Refine your destiny and establish a Living Yes mission statement.

Goal: Write two to five broad goals you are able to accomplish in the near term that will continue your Living Yes mission. While deciding how to describe each goal, consider how you will measure whether you have met the goal.

Objectives: Under each goal, write three or more specific tasks you will take to accomplish that goal.

Planning Tools Worksheet

Mission_____

_____

Goal #1 _____

      Objective#1_____

      Objective#2_____

      Objective#3_____

      Objective#4_____

      Objective#5_____

Goal #2 _____

      Objective#1_____

      Objective#2_____

      Objective#3_____

      Objective#4_____

      Objective#5_____

Goal #3 _____

      Objective#1_____

      Objective#2_____

      Objective#3_____

      Objective#4_____

      Objective#5_____

EXERCISE – TAKING ACTION ☒

Select seven key objectives from the planning tools worksheet, and rewrite them with space between each one.

Under each objective, write three to seven specific tasks you will do in the near future.

Put a "T" next to the tasks you will do *today* (or *this week*). Do these and continue to update your objectives as you move forward.

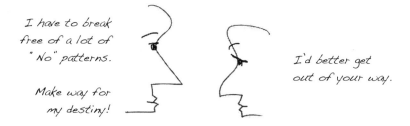

I have to break free of a lot of "No" patterns.

Make way for my destiny!

I'd better get out of your way.

SUPPORT

You can make a plan for effective help that will not burden your helpers.

Knowing that someone is present and cares about what you do is a powerful way to help you meet your goals. If you are supposed to be at work at 8:00 each morning, but no one cares when you show up, and there is no one depending on your services at 8:00 a.m., you are not likely to be on time. However, if you're needed at a team meeting, an appointment is scheduled, or even an office manager is checking their watch, you are more likely to show up on time. The social world is an effective tool in

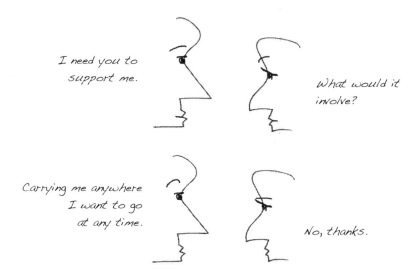

supporting you to behave.

How can you use this social world to help you keep your word to Live Yes without punishing yourself or burdening others? Here's an approach: Ask someone who cares about you to listen to you report whether you did what you said you would do. For example, you decide to save for a new mattress by putting $25 aside each week. Support yourself by asking a friend to read a brief text, email, or take a phone call each week that might say, "I saved twenty-five dollars!" It's that simple. Most people are more than willing to hear you update them on your progress.

The support person does not have to praise you, criticize you, lecture you, or reward you. They don't even have to remember to ask you. If they want to be a cheerleader and you like that, that's fine. What matters is that you have someone to hear (or read) your report who cares about your goal — even if you miss the target. All they have to do is listen or read whether or not you did what you set out to do. Giving support this way is easy and low pressure. Receiving it is powerful.

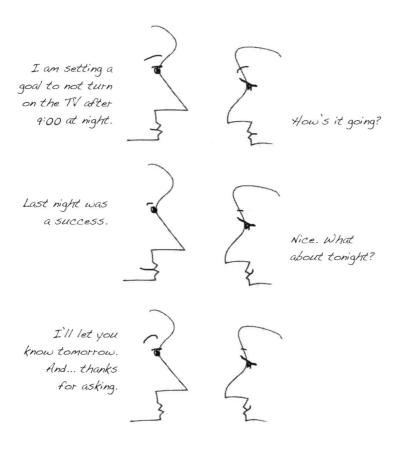

PROGRESS CHECK

What ways have you discovered to say "Yes" to pain in your life?

Where can you apply your unique destiny in your life?

What are your challenges?

What is the reason for you to overcome those challenges?

Are your goals clear enough to support your mission?

What tasks do you intend to do today?

How do they relate to your goals?

Who's on your support team? What are their roles?

Finding Peace

FEELING DEEPLY WITH BREATH—
SOME PRACTICAL IDEAS TO PRACTICE BEING MINDFUL

Remember to breathe!

Rikka Zimmerman once asked, "What would you do if you had only ten seconds to live?" If you react with a No, you'd panic and get stuck, but if you Live Yes, you would suddenly have no expectations and no demands. You could get out of your head and experience your life in a full, immediate, straight-in-your-face Yes. Now that would be living!

You can get ahead by getting out of your head. With practice, your mind can become quiet. You can learn to be still. Imagine a muddy glass of water. If you set it on the counter and don't move it, the mud will settle to the bottom and the water will become clear. Spiritual masters compare this stillness to a lake with no ripples, completely undisturbed, which perfectly reflects the moon above.

One way to reach this stillness is to focus on the breath. The next exercise guides you to quiet the mind with breathing.

EXERCISE — THREE STEPS TO BE IN THE PRESENT
THROUGH BREATH ☒

1. Identify the feeling (resulting from the thinking)
2. Identify the body sensations
3. Breathe repeatedly while concentrating on the physical sensations and feelings.

You may not think you need to learn to breathe, but yogis spend lifetimes perfecting one breathing technique.

Here are some breathing pointers.

Breathe slowly.

Breathe deeply. You often think you're breathing when you're not.

When your thoughts are racing, take in enough air.

Use breath to slow your thinking.

Trust that breathing and being present are all it takes.

Breathe all the way down into your lower back, belly, and sides.

When you inhale, expand your belly outward. When you exhale, pull in your belly.

At the point after you have no air in your lungs, relax. Take the next breath when it comes naturally, without forcing it.

Breathe out one more count than you breathe in.

Breathe in through your nose and out through your mouth.

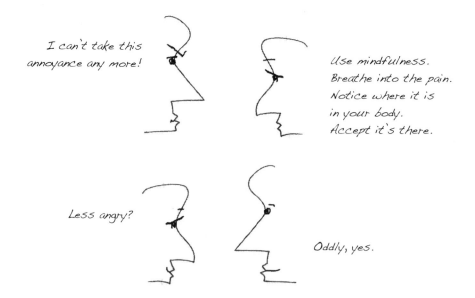

EXERCISE — GETTING DEEPER:
WAYS TO RELIEVE PENT-UP EMOTIONS ☒

Use breathing to feel. Emotional flooding can be reduced by being present, and the best way to be present is to focus on the breath. If you have thoughts, identify the feelings they cause. Pick the primary feeling: shame, sadness, anger, fear. Move up the scale from weak phrases like "I'm hurt" or "I'm upset" to stronger phrases like "I'm ashamed" to "I'm sad" then to "I'm angry" or "I'm anxious" and possibly to "I'm afraid." If you think you may soon feel something deeper that you don't feel yet, let yourself feel that anyway. For example, if you think you're angry but you don't feel it yet, then assume you're angry and breathe as you feel your anger. Focus on your breath. Let the emotion flow wherever it goes.

Use feeling to breathe. Breathe while concentrating on the feeling words. Be sure to witness both the in breath and the out breath. For example, if you have selected anger, concentrate on "I am feeling anger" as you breathe in and again as you breathe out. Do this for 60 seconds without another thought. Take at least three breaths in and three breaths out. If you find yourself thinking other thought-words or wanting to talk, go back to the feeling words while you breathe in and out. As Brad Brown would say, "Three conscious breaths will change the world."

Use movement or other physical motion to deepen the experience. Aerobic exercise is helpful. Aerobic means "living in air." Movement forces you to breathe. Moving to music is an easy and fun way to do aerobic movement. Another way is to expand your chest when you do the breathing exercise. Spread your arms open wide while you breathe into the feelings, feet flat on floor and shoulders pulled back. This will open your heart center. Especially if you have tightness or pain, use your healthy body energy as a resource for relief. While breathing, picture white light coming from your strong parts to fill the parts that hurt.

Or do this: Get in a comfortable place, close your eyes, and tighten your leg muscles for 10 seconds. Then release your muscles for 20 seconds. Now tighten your belly 10 seconds and then release your belly for 20 seconds. Now tighten your chest for 10 and release for 20 seconds, then tighten your arms for 10 and release for 20 seconds, and finally tighten your face for 10 and release for 20 seconds. You can also do this by creating a tightening wave starting at your feet and then moving to your head as you breathe in, then a loosening wave returning from your head to your feet as you breathe out.

EXERCISE — MOVING IN SPACE   ⊠

In loose clothes, walk around and experience your body in space. Be creative. Get out of your mind and into your movement. Increase your awareness of how your body flows.

Now, keeping the same awareness, imagine there is no gravity, and you are weightless. Keep moving. Then return to the earth for a while. Now imagine you are moving in warm, blue water. After a while, change to baby oil and keep moving. Now imagine you are moving in clean, green mud (like the volcanic mud used in facials). In time, change to wet cement. When ready, picture yourself in a solid diamond.

Stay aware of your body as it is held fixed by the solid diamond. Then return to the wet cement and move again. Go to the green mud for a while, to the baby oil for a while, to the blue water for a while. Each of these allows you to loosen in space. Now for a moment return to the air and then to weightlessness. After doing the weightlessness, return to the earth and move comfortably in the air.

Sit for a while and see how your body feels. It may be a good time to meditate or do something else relaxing.

~~~~~~

BEING AND DOING YES

Alternate between thought and action, saying "Yes" to both.

Dual means two. Duality is an old idea that looks at the two parts in everything: light & shadow, hot & cold, male & female. All thoughts have opposites. All existence has opposites. Duality is natural and normal.

One duality of Life is between doing and being. Doing is the masculine side. Being is the feminine. Doing is energy, force, drive, accomplishment. Being is form, the context, the container. For example, in the body, the male genitals are force (doing) and the female womb is form (being). The sex act is a symbol that shows this duality of force (doing) and form (being). In our activities, we shift between doing and being. As the old song goes: do be do be do....

Being and doing is where it's at.

Highly overrated.

What about thinking?

Live Yes in the moment and right here right now. The past is gone. If you don't let yourself get attached to a rigid view of the past, there is no cause for anger. This is true for memories of fifteen years ago, two weeks ago, and three seconds ago. The future has not yet happened. If you don't struggle to control the future, there is no need for worry. This is true for three seconds from now, two weeks from now, and fifteen years from now.

One technique to find stillness is to become fully aware of the present moment. This is called "mindfulness" or "insight meditation." No matter where you are or what you are doing, be fully present. If you're eating, eat. If you're working, work. If you're walking, walk. Experience Life through your senses as it is occurring right here and right now. This approach to Life is what the Buddhist's call "beginner's mind," where every experience is brand new and completely fresh. With practice, you will begin to experience a tender state with no disturbance, no anger, and no anxiety. It's a major part of Living Yes.

Without action, there is no movement. Living Yes requires action and fresh thinking. Mary Kay, the cosmetics queen, taught her staff "What you think about, you bring about." Doing means acting with direction. Acting with a values-centered direction is an important part of Living Yes.

So how do you know whether you are Living, Doing, and Being Yes or No? Answer: Feel when your sacred self is talking to you. Know when the reactive ego or false self is pretending it's the real self.

In the Bible, the "wicked one ... prowls around like a roaring lion." In the Quran, he "lies in wait." This fallen angel talks and sneaks around, pretending to be truthful. He often works in secret, in mystery, out of sight, unconsciously. In a modern context, this "devil talk" works in your own mind. If you blame yourself for this, you are trapped in No.

Put light onto the problem. Look at how this destructive energy tries to prove itself and manipulate you by creating splits. Dual thoughts of evil and good, temptation and bliss, wrong and right are entertaining, but they are sometimes false choices.

In context, truth is truth and lies are lies. Listen to your spiritual center, connect, and be present. Being present is Being Yes. Being Yes leads to Doing Yes. When you feel this True Self, you know that you are Living Yes in being and doing.

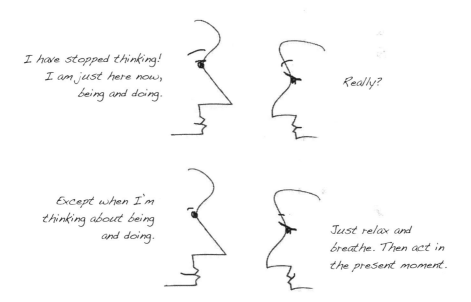

QUIETING YOUR MIND

Settle down and listen to the stillness.

Release stored energy by stretching and moving your body. Reduce the speed of your racing thoughts. Breathe. Find the seat of your soul with silence. Be in the moment. Listen to your heart. Sit in meditation. Find stillness. Practice ritual prayer. Relax. Live Yes and open yourself to your Higher Power. When you choose to find "the peace that passeth all understanding," the result is a deepening experience of the sacred voice discussed in Chapter Four.

Living Yes results in mental strength. Quieting the mind opens the Self to feel something greater than you can imagine. Manage your body and calm your mind with mental discipline. Develop the skill to stay ahead of your reactive mind. Will yourself to quiet thinking. Practice constant attention. Here is a technique to use.

EXERCISE — ENVIRONMENTAL AWARENESS   ☒

Quiet the mind by practicing being aware of the present moment without thinking thoughts from the past or the future. This can be done at any time in any place.

Begin by focusing on the physical senses. Concentrate on what you see, hear, touch, smell, taste. Is the sky bright? Can you hear the traffic in the distance? Is the air moist or dry? Can you smell the dirt on the street? What are the sensations in your mouth and on your tongue? Allow the full experience to flow, and notice what is happening.

This may be done easily with pleasurable, routine tasks such as cooking, sewing, gardening, fixing a sink, watching a sunset, walking by a brook, climbing a hill, having a massage, swimming, riding a bike, performing, making love. Just keep your mind on the sensations of the task.

With practice, you can do this at any time, including less pleasant experiences. For example, imagine you're at a job interview.

Concentrate on what is actually happening. What is the color and cut of the interviewer's blouse, the squeak of her chair as she leans back, the shape of her smile, the flow of her words, her facial expression, the feel of the cool, dry air-conditioning in the room, the lemon-ammonia smell of the table cleaner, the tangy taste of the complimentary soft drink?

Being present is all it takes to Live Yes. Let your thoughts fall away. Then listen, only listen. The result can reduce your anxiety and increase your awareness of Life. With practice, you can find a state of increased relaxation both in silence and in the most active parts of the world.

Chart – Where Do You Live?

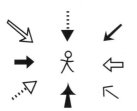

Secular outer world, reactive mind, noise, anger, accusations, demands, anxiety, worry, sadness, irritation, fear-based thinking

Spiritual inner world, allowing mind, stillness, quiet, calm, forgiving, allowing, bliss, inner joy, grace, no thinking, only being

Here are some actions to help you live in the spiritual inner world: Be willing to relax. Be completely quiet and still. Watch and be aware of your mind. Let the thoughts go by. Stay out of your head energy. Step back. Gently disengage from all thought. Float. Relax. Release. Accept. Surrender. Pass through. Let it go. Remain centered. Maintain present awareness. Be your true self. Pure consciousness. Deep. Inside.

We are in a sacred plane of joy, wholly fulfilled and Living Yes, when we are beyond sense, reason, or feeling. When we tune in with body and mind and accept signals of limitation, we discover the embrace of All-Is-Well. Through whatever method you know, seek the quiet part of you that exists behind thoughts. There you will find the silent truth.

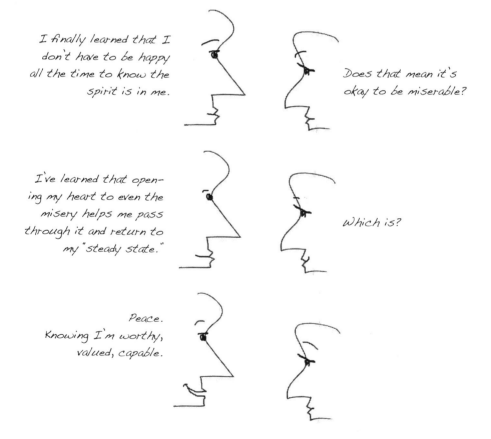

When we Live Yes, we can reject the chatter of our reactive mind and attend to the gift of opportunity. As we introduced in Chapter Four, the reactive mind is an endless loop of self-defeating talk. Instead of fighting the reactive mind with more reactive thoughts, choose the sacred light of knowing without any thought. Zero thought. Nada. The ultimate Yes. This is why inner peace can be found in silence. And silence can be found through meditation.

MEDITATING

Find the quiet within.

While we are practicing Living Yes in real time, we can continue to open our hearts to our Higher Power. If we pray without begging, and fully open ourselves in grateful conversations, we are reaching closer to Living Yes. Breathe, relax, settle the mind, and let the thoughts float away. Find inner quiet. Intentionally picture safe, relaxing places to reach stillness. All this is meditation. A student of mine observed: "Prayer is talking; meditation is listening."

Traditionally, meditation involves a strict posture (*asana*) and quieting the mind with a goal of total silence, inside and out. Much has been written and spoken about using meditation and breath to slow our minds. Various forms of meditation practice are taught in many religions. English-speaking authors such as Yogananda, Hanh, and Tolle offer wonderful access. Learning to meditate in this way is a long-term process that begins with small steps. The reward is to discover "the still small voice" behind your inner truth. You can find the place you have always known, Living Yes.

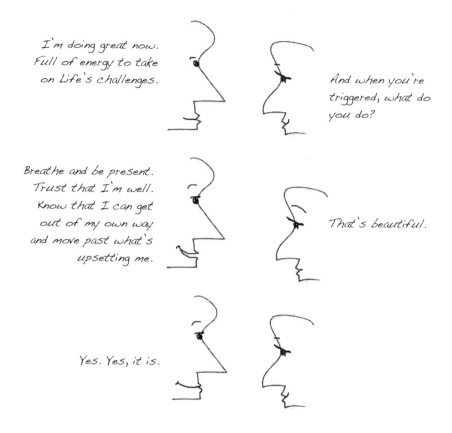

~~~~~~
EXERCISE — SILENT SITTING MEDITATION:
FIVE-PART TECHNIQUE   ☒
~~~~~~

Find your spiritual center with silence. Sitting meditation is a
direct path to your Higher Power, and there are many techniques
available to make this more successful and meaningful. Here are
some ideas, presented in five parts.

1. Prepare

Practice twice per day, even if you start at 1-3 minutes
each sitting.

Practice at the same times each day. Set the chair and room in a certain way each time. Perhaps use the same blanket or wear the same shirt. Rituals such as these will help your body and mind quickly remember that this is the time and place for sitting.

Stretch your muscles before you sit. Do it the same way each time. Stretches that begin with sitting on the floor are helpful. Basic *hatha* yoga postures are wonderful.

Sit on a comfortable, flat-seated chair, keeping the spine straight, jaw parallel to the floor, chest up and shoulders back, feet flat on the floor, arms gently resting on your lap. Sit up straight without letting your back touch the chair.

2. No thinking

Realize that the voice in your head is always working to pull you away from the silence. Win each battle with will and discipline. The longer and deeper you practice, the easier sitting in silence will become. Don't seek results. Keep persisting toward silence. Trust the Yes of the universe.

Notice. Let the judgments pass. Don't get caught up in analysis or problem solving. Just be; be here now.

If your mind is racing, take control. You can assert mentally, "Never mind my mind."

Seek silence. Allow your thoughts to pass by. Pretend they are floating away on clouds or they are signs on train cars rolling down the track into the distance, leaving you alone in the quiet mind.

3. Breathe

Here are five breathing techniques. Practice one at a time.

A. Watch the breath. Is it shallow or deep, fast or slow, rhythmic or uneven? Do not force the breath. Notice it. Follow it. Ease into it. Think "in" when the air is coming in and "out" when the air is going out. Notice if it changes on its own. Keep thinking "in" and "out." And then stop thinking.

B. Breathe in from the belly, not from the chest. Put your hand on your naval and feel your belly extend forward as you breathe in. When you breathe out, gently suck your belly back toward your spine. Hold for a comfortable length before breathing out. When you are ready, exhale fully. Clear your lungs completely before breathing in. When you have pushed out all the air, exhale even more. Sit with no air in your lungs. Don't inhale too soon.

C. Let yourself breathe. Let the muscles soften. Consciously allow yourself to soften, to relax. Say a phrase ("mantra") to yourself over and over such as "I am relaxed" or "I am peace" or "God loves me."

D. Use breath-counting techniques to get a rhythm. Here's a good one from Thich Nhat Hanh: Count "one" on the in breath, "one" on the out breath. "Two" on the in breath. "Two" on the out breath. "Three" on the in breath. "Three" on the out breath. All the way to "ten" on the in breath, "ten" on the out breath. Then repeat counting. "One" on the in breath, "one" on the out breath. Continue. Each time you reach "ten," return to "one."

E. An ancient Sufi technique is to breathe in thinking: "There is no God ..." And then breathe out thinking: "... but God." Repeat.

4. Deepen

Here are three deepening techniques.

A. Focus your breath on the heart center (center of chest at height of heart). This helps remove negative self-talk.

B. Find the physical location of the center of your Self at that moment, and put your finger there. Use breath to center your whole being there.

C. Imagine you are sitting inside your center. Or imagine your center is facing you. Look at it. Sense it. Breathe. Experience what is going on in your center. Take in what your center is offering. Relax. See if you can intuit how your center and your experience connect. Breathe. Relax.

Before you say to yourself, "This is impossible," "I can't sit that long," "No one can stop thinking that long," "This isn't worth it," "I'm the only one who can't do this," and the hundreds of other thoughts your reactive mind is hurling at you, go back to Chapter Four and use the techniques to clear your mind and relax. Accept that you do not have to be a perfect meditator. No one is. Do the best you can. Approach meditation by Living Yes. Trust your sacred self to know that you can do it. The results may surprise you!

THE PLEASURE PRINCIPLE

Pleasure results from thinking. Peace results from not thinking.

We are wired to seek pleasure (or avoid pain) through the firing of a chemical brain signal called "dopamine." This signal fires in the instinct part of our brain, located way in back and hidden from the front, logical, thinking part.

Feeling this dopamine pleasure leads to habit behaviors, large and small. Large habits may involve staying in your own misery, blaming others, always going along, mentally beating yourself, not keeping your word, indulging in drugs, alcohol, or other escape behaviors. Small habits may include eating an extra cookie, spilling the latest gossip, not walking when you can, going to bed too late, watching a little too much television, or buying a new pair of shoes that you don't need. As a whole, we do what feels good, what sells itself at the moment. We take the easy way, focusing on how to survive and fight through each day. To most of us, those surviving actions become the central part of our lives. We have slipped into living in an automatic No, and we have become unable to see the possibilities that Life is offering.

This is not to say there is anything wrong with seeking pleasure, just as there is nothing wrong with eating ice cream. But expecting pleasure to bring you closer to spirit is like thinking that ice cream is all you need to eat. The pursuit of pleasure is very different from the pursuit of peace. Pleasure comes from getting dopamine to fire. Peace comes from stillness.

Here's some good news: When we stop chasing after dopamine pleasures, something changes. We begin to slow down. We become less attached to the constant thought-chatter. We become more creative. We become more in touch with our experience of Reality. Instead of acting from our Fear, we act from our Truth. We become sure about being human, deal with whatever comes, take a stand on who we are, and in doing so, we discover how Life has been there to support us all along. We know that we do not have to chase dopamine. We know that by simply being, we are creating. When we do this, we feel the gift of each breath, and we become fully aware of the depth and beauty of each instant. Free of seeking pleasure, we experience peace. Even when we are not aware of it, the universe rewards us for Living Yes.

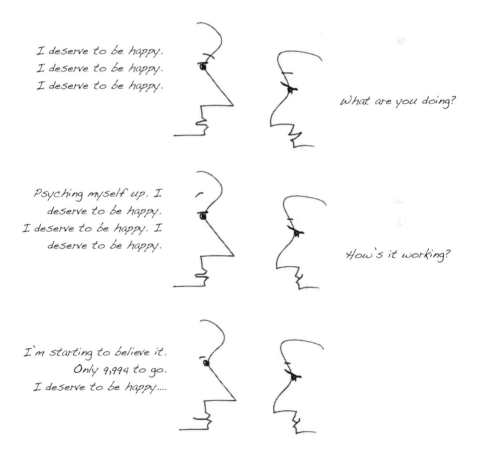

Take a moment to review the world(ly) voice / sacred voice list in Chapter Four (Chart – The Two Voices). The worldly struggles result from thoughts about chasing pleasure or running from pain. The sacred voice results from pursuing peace. As you practice the techniques in this book, you improve your ability to notice and let go of the thinking traps and the harmful things you do. Awareness and release will enable you to slow your thinking and live closer to Spirit.

A wise man offers this story: "When God built man, he had to find a place to hide the soul. He knew man had a habit of cutting everything into pieces. He needed a place to put the soul in the body that no knife could reach. So he put the soul inside the heart."

As you practice your version of spirituality, including the breathing and meditation techniques in this chapter, you will be able to glimpse the peaceful advantage of being present and heart-filled. With practice, this is a powerful way to slow your thoughts and learn who you are. Sometimes it is important to let the world take care of itself while you seek the sacred. Find a new type of awareness, one that does not depend on dopamine payoffs to meet false demands in your head, but instead links your heart and mind directly with what is Real.

EXERCISE — TEN WAYS TO BUILD LOVE   ⊠

1. Picture expanding your love for yourself.

2. Picture yourself expanding your love for others.

3. Open your heart to someone in need.

4. Practice seeing the world from others' points of view.

5. Remember a kindness (word, action, glance) that someone did for you.

6. Think of a great teacher in your life.

7. Think of someone who has been supportive.

8. Enjoy the love of babies, pets, colors, flowers, laughter, song, kindness.

9. Shift from what's missing or broken, and instead appreciate what is found and complete.

10. Feel the ember of love in your chest, and fuel it to expand into a roaring flame.

EXERCISE — TEN WAYS TO FEEL JOY ⊠

1. Concentrate on being right here, right now.

2. Quiet the mind enough to feel the rising wellspring of joy.

3. Be at least as quiet as the last time you were quiet.

4. Create each new moment of fresh Living Yes.

5. Warmly feel the beauty of helpful moments.

6. Feel alive in nature.

7. Enjoy physical movements, fully using sights, sounds, touches, tastes, smells, textures.

8. Experience the wonder and awe of the universe.

9. Experience gratitude for Life's gifts.

10. Experience freedom from having to possess any of those gifts.

PROGRESS CHECK

How have you used breathing to experience and move through your feelings?

Have you been able to experience a truthful knowing?

How can you (re)create that?

Can you quiet your mind for one or more minutes and feel the "still, small voice"?

If so, what is that experience like for you?

Are there areas in your life where you are eating only the ice cream instead of the whole meal?

In other words, are there areas where you are chasing pleasures at the cost of peace?

Are you choosing to use the tools offered to feel peace, love, and joy?

How does this help you to Live Yes in your daily life?

10   Putting It Together

REMEMBER BEING POSITIVE (THE POSITIVE ASSUMPTION)

Living Yes in real time, without being victimized by your reactive mind, is being positive.

At the opening of Chapter One, I asked you to forget being positive. But being positive, when grounded in Living Yes, is a choice just like any other choice. When being positive is seen as an ongoing choice, it has deep meaning. Living Yes in its pure form opens the world in a positive way. Living Yes allows hopefulness, faith, sunshine, open heart, infinite stillness, Father, Mother, Son, Daughter, Holy Spirit, Divine Love to flow through you. This is the way to Live Yes in real time, in the eternal now.

If you take a moment to review the contents of this book, you will see many aspects of being positive, such as setting boundaries, being willing, or listening to the quiet mind. Use these and other "positive" qualities as a measure to see whether your choices are helping you Live Yes. For example, are you making choices that are caring and compassionate, creative and connected, enriching and expansive, faithful and focused, generous and grateful, heroic and humble, inspired and intuitive, merciful and magnanimous, present and pure, relaxed and respectful, sincere and strong, trustworthy and truthful, watchful and wise? If so, you are probably enjoying Living Yes.

The only obstacle to being positive is your own self-doubt. A Japanese proverb says, "Fall seven times, stand up eight." That is how you exercise your free will. When you act from your deepest values, without destructive self-deception, you are taking a positive stand. Believing "I can do it" and telling someone else "You can do it!" helps too. Of course, it is not so easy to let the universal song flow in all moments. But it is certainly a state worth striving toward! Live, breathe, feel, and choose as both a cause and result of Living Yes.

If you think a situation is hopeless with no way out, you have lost your freedom to Live Yes. If you say or do something because you think your survival depends on it, you have lost your freedom to Live Yes. When you make yourself suffer to meet your co-created obligations or seek to satisfy others based on your desire to please, you have lost your freedom to Live Yes. When you get caught in any of the thinking traps discussed in Chapter Four, you have lost your freedom to Live Yes.

You can overcome those limits. You can create the freedom to Live Yes. Creativity is the ability to make change. Do creative things in response to a challenge. Look at what you want to accomplish, then see what you have and what you want to overcome. Break it into steps. Follow your destiny and mission statement. Create and Live Yes.

LIVING YES IN REAL TIME

Find the power in The Now.

Opening your heart to the flow of the universe is called "bliss" in the East and "rapture" in the West. Living Yes in real time is a challenge that many religions have helped many of us meet for thousands of years.

To Live Yes with each and every situation calls us to have faith, focus, and courage. Faith requires dedication to One Goal, always coming back to the Truth we know. Focus requires dedication to One Goal, always coming back to the Truth we know. Courage requires dedication to One Goal, always coming back to the Truth we know. Living Yes requires a dedication to that same One Goal and Truth.

By focusing on The Now and living with faith in what The Now offers, you can make courageous choices and Live Yes. By using what you've learned about Living Yes, you can choose a way of being that is not attached to the demands of your reactive mind. Instead, you can keep your Self close to the sacred Intelligent Force, upon the throne, the seat of the soul. Watch yourself react and pro-act while remaining open-hearted and taking your storyline lightly.

Remember how a hero walks? She feels the fear but still puts the next foot forward. Even while her heart is pounding, her breathing is heavy, and her eyes are tearing, she puts the next foot forward. As any combat soldier can report, courage is not a fearless walk into battle; it is a wobbly, weak-kneed walk into battle. How upright you stand, how calmly you breathe, how rested your mind stays does not matter as long as you do what you do. If you demand any other way, you are saying "No." Instead, make a decision, put one foot after the other, and engage Life. That's what it takes. Feel the fear while you keep going. That's courage. That's Living Yes.

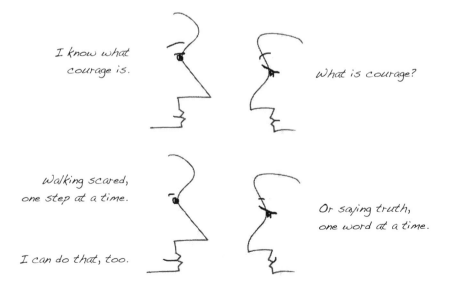

INTENTION AND FREEDOM

Make a choice to be free by Living Yes.

We ask kids to "look both ways before crossing the street," drivers to "keep your hands on the wheel and your eyes upon the road," and athletes to "keep your eye on the ball." All this advice is to help us do our tasks with a clear purpose. If we do everything right now, in the moment, we will Live Yes with full intention. To do anything less is to say "No." Buddhist Jack Kornfield writes, "Don't think. Experience."

Consider the words of a wise student of mine: "Every challenge we have is a test of our ability to be where we have to be." Any time we make efforts to control a situation, we are trying to manipulate the future. The result is that we are saying "No" to Life as it is.

One test to see if you are Living Yes is to check if your thoughts are in the present. If you are being anxious and worrying about what might happen, you are not present and not Living Yes. If you are annoyed, irritated, or stuck looking backward to the past, you are not present and not Living Yes. To Live Yes when you face a challenging situation, remain aware of your avoidance but don't give in to it. Set clear boundaries and choose to Live Yes, right then and there.

No matter what is happening to you outside, your freedom comes from within. A happy man in prison is freer than a self-deluded fool in the world. The old idea that "Discipline brings you freedom" works. When you have the intention to act in a disciplined way, you will accomplish what you set out to do. This is being your true self. This is mental freedom. This is the freedom that comes with Living Yes.

Integrity means having all of your parts work as one. Telling the truth and living up to your promises keeps you whole, sure, and consistent. If you do what you say you are going to do, you are not allowing yourself to break into Yes and No parts. When you do not get trapped by worldly thinking, you hold your faith and your integrity. With integrity you are one with yourself and your world.

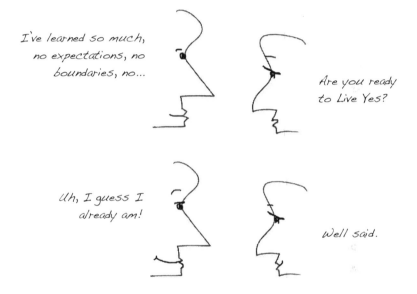

Chart – Choosing from Reality (next page)

As shown in the Four Stages of Moving from No to Yes chart at the end of Chapter Two, every event we face offers us the choice to Live Yes or Die No. This final chart illustrates this ongoing process, while summarizing the major concepts in this book. Use it as a tool to Live Yes in your daily life.

As each situation arises, compare the choices of moving forward (Living Yes) or moving backward (stuck in No). Then start all over again.

STUCK

fate

predetermined

previous beliefs

self-righteousness,
  selfish, ego

position

repeating behaviors

habit

worldly voice, noise

past- or future-oriented

believing the lies

avoiding discomfort

blinded by secondary gain

RESIST

expect

demand

accuse, judge

complain, criticize, gossip

denial of possibilities

gratified by fulfilled expectations

unwilling to risk

lonely

  impossibility   thinking traps:

  survival   all or nothing thinking

  obligation   judging

  desire to please   jumping to conclusions

                             emotional reasoning

DEFEND

reactive mind

predictable

disengaged

stilted living

having to please

rigid No, dying No

persecutor, victim,
  rescuer

downward cycle

aggressive, passive,
  passive-aggressive

disconnected

separated

stiff and suffocating
unconscious
unaware
all head, no body
indulging imagination

react, automatic
self-delusion
holding on, always afraid
mind sees effect
unconscious, entranced,
  asleep, numb

Moving backward

NO ← STA

SPECIFIC SITUATIONS

RECEIVE

human
real, lovable
open-hearted emotion
compassion
undreamed-of possibility
willingness
support
freedom
accepting
learning from Life
using separating
  emotion to change
love and joy

INSPIRE

destiny
unfolding Life
clear thinking
humility, gratitude
psychological flexibility
ever-fresh responses
reveal sacred self in the
  moment, The Now
fun with challenges
knowing the truth
healthful detachment
take your storyline lightly

loose and expanding
consciously breathing
conscious
aware of surroundings
moving in space

CREATE

proactive mind
being Yes and
  doing Yes
engaged
humble, knowing
Grace
Life fully lived
creative looping
set clear boundaries
assertive
connected, whole
live by values

reflect, choose
ongoing processing
reject the No, assert the Yes
letting go, trust faith
mind sees cause
indentify and refute
  thinking traps
  and core lies
alternative thinking

RT ➔ **YES**

Moving forward

TRIGGERS

EVENTS

WHO ARE WE REALLY?

Meaning is revealed by being human.

How do we become fully human? What do our lives mean? Who are we, really? Those questions have been argued and ignored since humans became self-aware. They have been the subject of religion, philosophy, psychology, medicine, and science.

By Living Yes, we learn that Life is here to teach us what it means to be human. Living Yes reveals meaning. When we Live Yes, we tap into our higher self, our soul, and we learn how to accept the many lessons of Life.

Live Yes by noticing what is happening when the world is shaking you. You often find that you are not using your genius to tap into your divine nature. That's when you can catch yourself trapped in No. That's when it's time to make a 180-degree turn and Live Yes.

The word *genius* was used more than 800 years ago to mean "the divine nature that is present in all of us." By Living Yes, you fulfill yourself as a genius. You unlock the genie within. You have potential to tap into your divine nature and be a genius.

Living Yes is a process, not a result. There is no human who can Live Yes in real time all the time. The best you can do is to choose again and again and again to Live Yes.

WHAT IS LIVING YES?

What you now know.

By this point, you probably have a good idea of what Living Yes means. Here is one definition:

Living Yes is an active approach to living that is rooted in courageous truth-telling about our basic lovability. Every human context offers us the choice to reveal sacred joy and peace. When we use our knowledge to rise above the illusion of separation, we experience an open-hearted gratitude, an unceasing energy, and a spontaneous celebration of our oneness with All.

PROGRESS CHECK

Is the way you practice Living Yes about being positive, or is it more than that?

If more, what more is there for you?

What have you learned about being in The Now in your life?

What do you know about freedom and willingness that you did not know before?

What does it mean for you to be human?

How is meaning in your life being revealed?

What do you now know that you didn't know when you started to understand and practice Living Yes?

Detailed Contents

Introduction: Living Yes or Dying No?

ARE YOU LIVING YES OR DYING NO?   2
What have you been taught?

BEING HUMAN   3
Human is what I am. No more. No less.

ABOUT THE BOOK   5
How does this book work?

THE LIVING YES PRINCIPLES   8
What is Living Yes?

PROGRESS CHECK   10

Chapter One: How to Live Yes

FORGET BEING POSITIVE   11
You can't be real if you fake it.

ZERO EXPECTATIONS   13
Unmet expectations result in frustration. Instead, expect nothing.

AM I A SELFISH KNOW-IT-ALL?   15
The more you think you know, the less you can learn.

EXPECTATIONS AND REALITY   16
When reality does not meet your expectations, you become annoyed.

THE PAST IS GONE   18
If you are present, you can give up all expectations.

EXPECTATIONS AND GOALS   19
Expectations are not goals.

EXPECTATIONS AND SPECULATION ABOUT THE FUTURE   21
Expectations block you from future possibilities.

☒ **EXERCISE – TWENTY-TWO WAYS TO PLAY AT LIVING YES.**   22

PROGRESS CHECK   24

Chapter Two: Learning Acceptance

BEING RIGHT   25
You have the right to remain willing.

ACCEPTANCE IS THE ANSWER   26
Acceptance is not the same as giving in.

ACCEPTING LIFE ON LIFE'S TERMS, EVEN WHEN IT'S HARD   27
Sometimes acceptance means learning how to be uncomfortable.

☒ **EXERCISE—THE ACCEPTANCE PROCESS**   29

ACCEPTANCE AND SPIRIT   31
Acceptance opens you to spirit.

DYNAMICALLY LIVING YES   32
There is not a Yes or No answer. Life doesn't stand still.
Living Yes is an ongoing challenge and opportunity.

☒ **EXERCISE—THE OPPOSITE VALUES PROCESS**   35

👁 **CHART—FOUR STAGES OF MOVING FROM NO TO YES**   37

PROGRESS CHECK   39

Chapter Three: Setting Boundaries and Sticking with Them

COST/BENEFIT OF SETTING BOUNDARIES   40
You can be nice and say "No." The result will be respect.

☒ **EXERCISE—**
   THE THREE-STEP MODEL FOR SETTING BOUNDARIES   42

BEING ASSERTIVE   43
Assertive behavior is honest and clear.

OVERCOMING RESISTANCE TO SETTING BOUNDARIES   44
Weakness is not the same as niceness.

👁 **CHART—AGGRESSIVE, PASSIVE,**
   PASSIVE-AGGRESSIVE, ASSERTIVE BEHAVIORS   45

👁 **CHART—ASSERT YOUR RIGHTS**   49

CONTROL ROLES   50
Don't be a persecutor, victim, or rescuer.

PROGRESS CHECK   52

Chapter Four: The Voice in Your Head

THE TWO VOICES   53
The little chatterbox in your head is a big liar.

⊠ **EXERCISE – WRITING THE SELF-TALK**   53

👁 **CHART—THE TWO VOICES**   57

HEARING THE WORLDLY VOICE   58
Practice noticing how your thoughts are not you.

⊠ **EXERCISE – THE THOUGHT RECORD PROCESS**   59

THINKING TRAPS   62
Your mind can trick you.

THE FOUR THINKING TRAPS   64
Break it down into four types.

THOUGHT RECORDS AND THE FOUR THINKING TRAPS   65
Presenting the master cognitive process.

⊠ **EXERCISE – DEVELOPING ALTERNATIVE THOUGHTS**   69

PROGRESS CHECK   73

Chapter Five: Feelings and Thoughts

WHAT IS A FEELING?   74
Understanding human architecture begins with learning
the difference between thinking and feeling.

👁 **CHART—THOUGHTS VERSUS FEELINGS**   75

⊠ **EXERCISE – THOUGHTS VERSUS FEELINGS QUIZ**   75

USING THE DIFFERENCE BETWEEN THOUGHTS AND FEELINGS   78
Thoughts often lie. Feelings never lie.

👁 **CHART—INTENSITY OF FEELINGS**   79

⊠ **EXERCISE – PRACTICE IDENTIFYING FEELINGS**   80

THOUGHTS PRODUCE FEELINGS 81
Use the principle of cognitive theory.

SEPARATED OR CONNECTED 83
Feelings can be connecting or separating and can teach us what we care about.

👁 **CHART—THE MOMENT MODEL** 86

⊠ **EXERCISE—THREE PLACES NOES LEAD AND
TRACING IT BACK TO GET TO YES** 87

DRILLING DOWN 89
Underneath the mind chatter are hidden lies.

👁 **CHARTS—HIDDEN THOUGHTS MODEL AND
HIDDEN THOUGHTS EXAMPLE** 89

DOWN TO THE CORE 91
One day you taught yourself a lie that colored your world.
Now it has turned you against yourself.

⊠ **EXERCISE—THE EIGHT CORE LIES (WAYS TO SAY "NO")
WITH TRUTH RESPONSE AFFIRMATIONS (LIVING YES)** 92

PROGRESS CHECK 94

Chapter Six: Feeling Emotions

ANGER HURTS 95
Anger is a painful way to prove you're right.

ANGER MANAGEMENT (THE FIRST STEP) 95
Let go of anger.

⊠ **EXERCISE—RELEASING ANGER** 97

ANGER PREVENTION (THE SECOND STEP) 98
Live Yes before you choose anger.

ALONE AND AFRAID, ANXIETY AND STRESS 100
The more you struggle to control your future, the more pain you will feel.

LIVING WITH COMPASSION 102
Live Yes with an open and vulnerable heart.

THE ANNOYED-WORRY CYCLE 104
Break the pattern with acceptance.

⊠ **EXERCISE—USING SEPARATING EMOTIONS TO
CHANGE YOUR THINKING** 106

BEING AND DOING NO   112
You struggle to prove to the world that you're okay.

👁 CHART—THE LOOPING TRAP (VICIOUS CYCLE)   113

👁 CHART—THE LOOP OF CORE LIES (ACCUSATIONS)
AND DRIVEN BEHAVIORS (DEMANDS)   114

CREATIVE LOOPING   117
Find the truth loop.

👁 CHART—THE TRUTH LOOP (VIRTUOUS CYCLE)   117

☒ EXERCISE—CREATE A TRUTH LOOP   117

PROGRESS CHECK   118

Chapter Seven: Patterns of No

AVOIDANCE: DIVIDE AND CONQUER NOTHING   119
Avoidance is a short-term strategy that fails over time.

BALANCING USEFUL AVOIDANCE   121
Avoidance is measured by intention.

PTSD   123
Post-traumatic stress is the No of avoidance.

☒ EXERCISE—CHANGING FROM NO TO YES
USING THE FIVE PRACTICES: NOTICES, FAITH,
KNOWLEDGE, ACTION, CONTINUING GRATITUDE   124

JUDGMENT   126
Judgment is not your job.

👁 CHART—BIG JUDGMENT WORDS LIST   127

HABITS, STUCK IN ME   129
Habits may trap you into blind pathways.

SECONDARY GAIN   130
We miss the Yes because of false payoffs.

☒ EXERCISE—THE SECONDARY GAIN PROCESS   132

☒ EXERCISE—TWO-COLUMN COST/BENEFIT PROCESS   133

PROGRESS CHECK   136